Mı
1 I
NE
NE

B A T T L E F I

NORTHUMBRIA
AT WAR

Etal Castle, surrendered to James IV before the Battle of Flodden. See pages 109 and 122.

BATTLEFIELD BRITAIN

NORTHUMBRIA
AT WAR

DEREK DODDS

Pen & Sword
MILITARY

For June

First published in Great Britain in 2005 by
PEN & SWORD MILITARY
an imprint of
Pen & Sword Books Limited
47 Church Street
Barnsley, South Yorkshire
S70 2AS

Copyright © Derek Dodds, 2005

ISBN: 1 84415 149 2

The right of Derek Dodds to be identified as
Author of this Work has been asserted by him in accordance
with the Copyright, Designs and Patents Act 1988.

A CIP catalogue record for this book
is available from the British Library

Designed and typeset in 9pt Palatino
by Sylvia Menzies, Pen & Sword Books Limited

Printed and bound in England by
CPI UK

Pen & Sword Books incorporates the imprints of
Pen & Sword Aviation, Pen & Sword Maritime,, Pen & Sword Military,
Wharncliffe Local History, Pen & Sword Select,
Pen & Sword Military Classics and Leo Cooper

For a complete list of Pen & Sword titles please contact:
PEN & SWORD BOOKS LIMITED
47 Church Street, Barnsley, South Yorkshire, S70 2AS, England
email: enquiries@pen-and-sword.co.uk
website: www.pen-and-sword.co.uk

Contents

NORTHUMBRIA

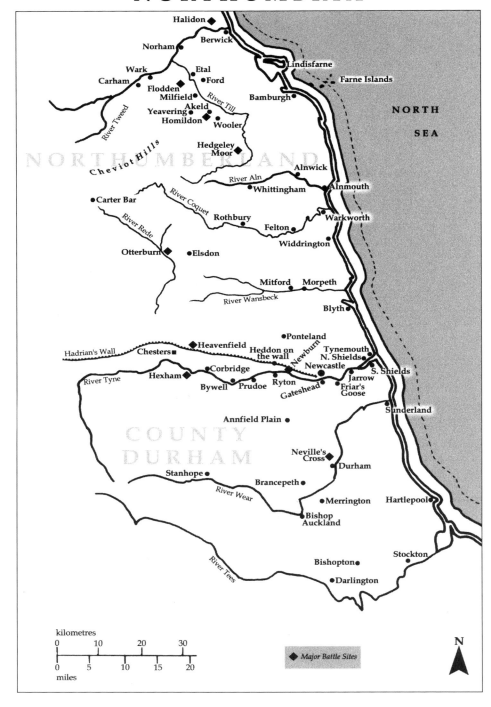

Halidon ◆
Norham ●
Berwick ●
Wark ●
Carham ●
Etal ●
Ford ●
Flodden ◆
Milfield ●
Akeld ●
Yeavering ●
Homildon ◆
Wooler ●
Lindisfarne
Farne Islands
Bamburgh ●

NORTH

SEA

Hedgeley Moor ◆

N O R T H U M B E R L A N D

Cheviot Hills

River Tweed
River Till

Alnwick ●
River Aln
Whittingham ●
Alnmouth ●

Carter Bar ●
River Coquet
Rothbury ●
Felton ●
Warkworth ●
River Rede
Widdrington ●

Otterburn ◆
Elsdon ●

Mitford ●
Morpeth ●
River Wansbeck
Blyth ●

Ponteland ●
Hadrian's Wall
Chesters ■
Heavenfield ◆
Heddon on the wall
Newburn
Tynemouth ●
N. Shields ●
Newcastle ●
S. Shields
Corbridge ●
Hexham ◆
River Tyne
Bywell ●
Prudoe ●
Ryton ●
Gateshead ●
Jarrow ●
Friar's Goose ●

Sunderland

Annfield Plain ●

C O U N T Y

D U R H A M

Neville's Cross ◆
Durham ●
Stanhope ●
Brancepeth ●
River Wear
Merrington ●
Hartlepool ●
Bishop Auckland ●

River Tees
Bishopton ●
Stockton ●
Darlington ●

kilometres
0   10   20   30

0   5   10   15   20
miles

◆ *Major Battle Sites*

N

Introduction &
Acknowledgements

Northumbria's history has marched to the drumbeat of war. Once part of an ancient kingdom, Northumbria is now popularly regarded as the land between the rivers Tweed and Tees, enclosing the original borders of Northumberland and Durham. For over a thousand years, armies have marched to battle across their hills and moors. During much of that time these historic northern counties have been a prisoner of their own geography. Caught in a struggle between emerging nations, the northern border in particular became an area of almost ceaseless military activity which spilled across the counties and down through the centuries. And even when war was officially over, strife persisted and added to the roll-call of battles, both famed and forgotten, in a Northumbria at War.

This volume is a narrative of that long conflict, drawing heavily upon original sources. Such ancient voices, however, despite their relative immediacy, have well-known limitations. For the earliest eras especially, their accounts can be brief and partisan, making difficult the detailed reconstruction of even major battles. These vibrant echoes of the past are nevertheless indispensable and are supplemented in this work by the scholarship of many later historians and a consideration of battlefield landscape wherever it survives.

In this respect, Northumbria is a treasure trove of discovery for the military historian. Northumberland above all, because of its persisting rural nature, has remained comparatively unscathed. It contains an extraordinary legacy of fortified sites and battlegrounds. They offer both scenic attractions and invaluable benefits to the historical explorer investigating their turbulent past. But despite this and even acknowledging the usefulness of A H Burne's oft-quoted concept of 'Inherent Military Probability', the final interpretation of what actually took place in these momentous locations must necessarily remain a personal view. As more modern and well-documented warfare has demonstrated, the improbable in battle does occur.

Many people have contributed to the production of this book. To those not mentioned I offer apologies and thanks in equal measure. In particular I must thank Andrew Dodds and Lynsey Ewan for their fine cartography and artwork which I only hope may be emulated by the text. Mr John Wilks, MA, formerly senior curator with Tyne and Wear Museum Service, kindly read my manuscript in various drafts and made helpful suggestions for its improvement. Thanks also to Lindsay Allason-Jones of Newcastle's Museum of Antiquities and Lesley Webster at the British Museum, who corrected my misconceptions on post-Roman history. Similarly, Hugh Cheape of the National Museums of Scotland and Philip Lankester at the Royal Armouries in Leeds fielded questions patiently and with good humour on Scottish heraldry and medieval weapons respectively. Notwithstanding this wealth of support, any shortcomings in the final publication are entirely my responsibility. Finally, to my wife June is owed the greatest debt of all. Countless hours of domestic neglect have tested her forbearance to the limit. Perhaps dedicating this book to her will mark a beginning to my rehabilitation.

In a recent work, a military historian has cautioned against attempting a more detailed analysis across such a broad span of Northumbrian history. It is left for the reader to judge how far I should have heeded his warning.

Chronology

AD 43	Major Roman invasion of Britain
122–136	Construction of Hadrian's Wall
547	Ida leads Angle tribes to begin establishment of Northumbrian kingdom
635	Battle of Heavenfield
642	Death of King Oswald at Battle of Oswestry
698–721	Lindisfarne Gospels written and illuminated
793	Viking attacks lead to fall of Northumbria
1006–1018	Malcolm II of Scotland invades the North
1066	William the Conqueror crowned King of England
1067	Assassination of Copsig, Earl of Northumbria
1069	Norman force commanded by Robert de Comines destroyed in Durham
1069	'Harrying of the North'
1080	Bishop Walcher murdered at Gateshead
1080	Odo of Bayeux ravages Northumbria
1093	Foundation of Durham Cathedral
1093	Malcolm III (Canmore) of Scotland killed at Alnwick
1095	Rebellion of Robert de Mowbray
1136	David II of Scotland campaigns in Northumbria
1138	Scottish defeat at Battle of Standard in Yorkshire
1139	Second Treaty of Durham
1141–1144	Scottish Chancellor William Cumin attempts to usurp Durham bishopric
1174	William I (the Lion) of Scotland captured at Alnwick
1237	Treaty of York
1296	Edward I captures Berwick and War of Scottish Independence begins
1297	Scottish victory at Stirling Bridge and invasion of Northumbria by William Wallace
1305	Wallace captured and executed

1314	Battle of Bannockburn
1314	Forces of Robert I (Bruce) of Scotland increase raids into Northumbria
1327	Weardale campaign of Edward III
1333	Battle of Halidon Hill
1346	English victory at Battle of Crécy during Hundred Years War
1346	Battle of Neville's Cross
1388	Battle of Otterburn
1402	Battle of Homildon (Humbleton) Hill
1415	Battle at Yeavering, Northumberland
1415	Battle of Agincourt
1455	St Albans, opening battle in Wars of the Roses
1461	Lancastrian defeat at Towton
1464	Battle of Hedgeley Moor and death of Ralph Percy
1464	Battle of Hexham
1464	Fall of Bamburgh and failure of Lancastrian campaign in the North
1482	Final transfer of Berwick to English control
1502	Signing of 'Treaty of Perpetual Peace'
1509	Accession of Henry VIII
1513	'Ill Raid' at Milfield near Wooler
1513	Battle of Flodden and death of James IV of Scotland
1544	English invasion of Scotland known as the 'Rough Wooing'
1547	Scottish defeat at Battle of Pinkie
1575	Raid of the Reidswire
1603	Union of the Crowns
1639	First Bishops' War
1640	Second Bishops' War and Battle of Newburn
1640	Treaty of Ripon
1642	Charles I raises standard at Nottingham to begin English Civil War
1644	Defeat of Royalists at Marston Moor
1644	Siege of Newcastle
1649	Execution of Charles I
1688	The Glorious Revolution
1691	French privateers raid coast of Northumberland
1715	First Jacobite rebellion
1716	Earl of Derwentwater executed
1745	Second Jacobite rebellion
1746	Destruction of Gateshead House
1746	Battle of Culloden
1761	Hexham Riot
1832	'Battle' of Friar's Goose
1832	Murder of Nicholas Fairless followed by conviction and execution of William Jobling
1914	War declared against Germany
1918	Death of Sergeant Pilot Joyce
1918	Armistice signed to end First World War

Roman power in north-east Britannia: remaining lower courses of Hadrian's Wall at Heddon-on-the-Wall.

Reconstructed Roman gatehouse at South Shields. The fort of Arbeia was built in AD 158 to defend the harbour and provide a supply depot for the Wall and its garrisons.

Courtesy of Tyne and Wear Museums

Chapter 1

KINGDOM IN CONFLICT
43–1066

On then into battle and as you go think both of your ancestors and your descendants. Tacitus, 2nd century AD

From the early history of Northumbria, little evidence remains of any large-scale military conflict. As Imperial Rome strengthened its grip on the green and damp isle of Britannia, any resistance in the North was probably spasmodic and regarded more as an irritation than a threat to the viability of the Roman presence. Even so, the British warrior established a reputation for toughness and a reckless determination which caused major setbacks to the Roman conquest.

Isolated and lightly armed northern tribes were more likely to engage in opportunist guerrilla raids but were eventually reconciled to Roman domination. Trade has always been a less dangerous pursuit than terror, and any impulse from the indigenous population towards resistance must have often seemed futile in the face of iron-clad infantry, bristling with weapons, who tramped in formation across their tribal lands.

Certainly Tacitus, the eloquent chronicler of Imperial expansion in this period, dismissed the severity of any north-eastern threat and concentrated instead on the opposition of woad-daubed Picts, who were finally crushed in a decisive battle as they retreated desperately to the ramparts of their Caledonian stronghold. It was only when the Legions had left to defend their crumbling empire in the east that the northern region began to struggle fitfully towards a separate identity. It was an identity forged in the burning crucible of battle.

By the sixth century, a tribe of Danish Angles led by Ida had braved the North Sea to eventually colonise parts of the north-east coast and occupy the forbidding shoreline defences at Bamburgh. Most of these ancient chiefdoms depended for their survival on the sword arm of their leader, and his death in combat consequently marked the collapse of his regime and the loss of his territory. However, Ida fought skilfully enough to successfully resist the Celtic threat which surrounded him and he lived long enough to lay down the foundations for the Kingdom of Northumbria, a vast area stretching from the Humber to the Forth.

> *Warriors mustered. They met together,*
> *With a single intention they attacked.*
> Celtic Heroic Poem, eighth century

Only vague and legendary memories remain of this battle for survival. These embryonic British states had few established literary traditions. Their history was instead woven into bardic stories which were passed down through the generations. Local place-names such as Battleshield Haugh may now bear a last faint echo of long-distant clashes of arms. But Heavenfield in Northumberland is a battlefield grounded on firmer historical foundations.

At Heavenfield, in the shadow of Hadrian's great Wall, a threatened Northumbrian kingdom was given life and a chance to prosper. The battle site crowns a small plateau on the gently rising slopes of the broad Tyne valley, barely five miles directly north of the modern market town of Hexham. The battlefield was largely unscathed by the construction of General Wade's military road which skirts closely past it and is a serenely peaceful spot with sweeping views towards a Northumberland upland of wild beauty. Yet once, it seems that this place of solitude was torn by the raucous din of battle horns and bellowing war chants.

> *The place is near the wall in the North by which the Romans once shut off the whole of Britain from the sea to prevent the attacks of the barbarians.* Bede, eighth century

In 635 at Heavenfield, pagan banners were unfurled, sword hilts were hammered on shields, and two native war bands faced each other to settle their fate in blood. Three years earlier at the battle of Hatfield Chase near Doncaster, the ferocious Welsh chieftain Cadwallon had smashed a Northumbrian army and killed Edwin its king. Military prowess combined with astute dynastic alliances had allowed Edwin to establish a kingdom which he oversaw from a warren of hill forts at Gefrin, known now as Yeavering, in the Cheviot Hills. But his untimely death meant that the kingdom of Northumbria now lay outstretched and vulnerable before the mighty Celtic warlord Cadwallon.

Leading the defence of his country was the new young king Oswald, a remarkable member of the Northumbrian aristocratic warrior caste who appears to have been as schooled in the Gospels as he was in sword play. If accounts of his greatest battle are to be accepted, Oswald's strategic guile and prowess as a military commander far outweighed his tender years, for it is claimed he selected his fighting ground before giving battle. By assessing the battlefield today, his good judgement can still be appreciated. Resting on a high ramp of land, Heavenfield is an ideal battle location. It is wedged between rocky outcrops on the northern and western flanks, and protected to the south by Hadrian's Wall

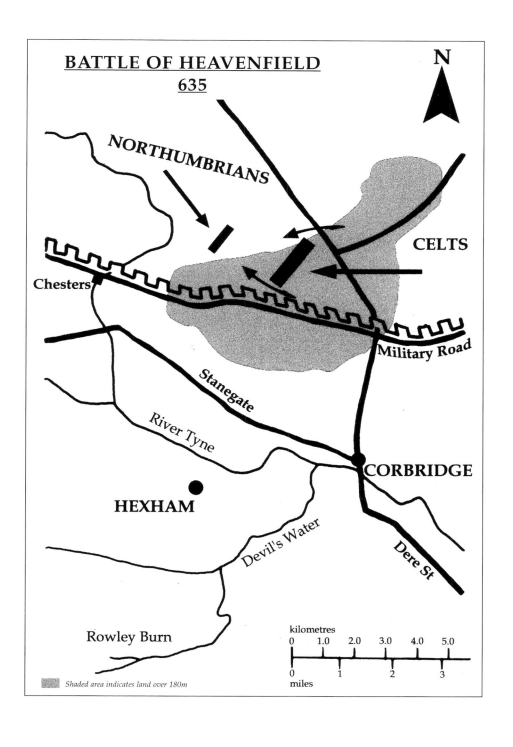

BATTLE OF HEAVENFIELD
635

N

NORTHUMBRIANS

CELTS

Chesters

Military Road

Stanegate

River Tyne

HEXHAM

CORBRIDGE

Devil's Water

Dere St

Rowley Burn

Shaded area indicates land over 180m

kilometres
0   1.0   2.0   3.0   4.0   5.0

0   1   2   3
miles

and its defensive ditch which in the seventh century would still have presented a formidable barrier.

Another legacy of Roman occupation may have played a significant role in this battle. Their sophisticated network of roads continued in use long after their departure and would have been vital for relatively speedy troop movements. Stanegate from the west, Dere Street from the south, and particularly the sinisterly named 'Devil's Causeway' which sliced diagonally across the region, were arteries of communication which led to Heavenfield. Cadwallon probably advanced north from his York stronghold along Dere Street, approaching its crossroads with Stanegate at the Northumbrian settlement of Corbridge where the River Tyne could be forded. His objective may have been to strike at the Northumbrian military base at Bamburgh as he continued north, crossing the Wall before becoming aware of an enemy force in the vicinity.

Seeking to draw Cadwallon away, Oswald's troops could then move from their encampment to form up on Heavenfield, where they prepared to withstand the shock of the Welsh onslaught. In this battlefield scenario the trap was sprung and Oswald held open its jaws. Turning westward, the battle-hardened Cadwallon then bore eagerly down upon his waiting adversary.

> *Oswald advanced with an army small, but strengthened with the faith of Christ.* Bede, eighth century

As far as can be known, Dark Age battles were probably short but extremely savage clashes with no hint of quarter. Before fighting began, however, both sides may have faced each other to trade insults instead of blows, enacting a ritual still observed in the behaviour of urban street gangs today. It remains as effective as ever to instil collective confidence and intimidate opponents into hasty and uncoordinated attacks.

Scenting victory against an outnumbered opponent and an untried leader, Cadwallon's warriors could then hurl themselves forward. Prior to this, to open the battle, there was possibly an exchange of slingshot and spears, weapons likely to have been favoured by most ordinary tribesmen of this period. Judging by the finely wrought sword blades that have been unearthed, metal working was a highly developed skill during this period. It is likely, though, that heavy battle swords, long axes and rudimentary but still expensive armoured protection would have been available only to the elite cadre of warriors who gathered around their leader. Most of the remaining war band would have been equipped with spears, axes and even simple farming implements. Some of these weapons may have been light and seemingly innocuous, but without doubt they would prove to be just as lethal in the brutal close-quarter combat into which these murderous encounters doubtless descended.

But as the Celts swarmed towards the Northumbrian line of battle, Oswald's choice of battleground was vindicated. A broad mass of Welsh tribesmen would be squeezed into a narrow front by the contours of the land over which they charged. As with many sites of battle, topography could decisively affect the final outcome. At Heavenfield, Cadwallon's momentum would be checked and his warriors tired by their ascent of the long rising slope which was defended by Oswald's army. Because of this it was possibly here, on the crest where a small

St Oswald's at Heavenfield. On the site of early Northumbria's most important battle.

church now stands, that the first wave of the Celtic attack broke upon a wall of closely packed Northumbrian defenders.

Powerful but increasingly desperate Celtic attacks could then be blunted by the Northumbrian shield wall. To be effective it had to be locked tightly against the wedge of struggling warriors who slashed and cut at it. Shields of this period were robustly constructed from hide-covered wood and many of them may have been strengthened significantly by the addition of a central iron boss. This was probably smaller than the Roman model but it was equally effective in deflecting sword blows and forcing back opponents.

Steadily, Oswald's men must have gained the upper hand as their assailants began to falter. Seizing the moment, the Northumbrian front rank could then spring forward and cut down the tiring warriors before them. At some stage of the bitter fighting, as always in battle, a critical turning point undoubtedly arrived. But whatever had caused the fatal loss of impetus, for Cadwallon the fight was effectively lost.

His routed men were said to have streamed away from the battlefield pursued by a bloodthirsty enemy. Many Celts were overtaken and killed in their headlong flight towards the south, including Cadwallon and his clansmen, who were overwhelmed as they attempted to escape across a stream. Two local waterways are associated with the death of the legendary Celtic warlord: Devil's Water, a fast-flowing tributary of the River Tyne, and Deniseburn or Rowley Burn which is further to the south in what is now County Durham.

Scant evidence other than local tradition has set the death of Cadwallon in these locations. A near contemporary description of the battle itself was written by Bede, the monkish scholar and first truly English historian. Although it was written barely within a century of Heavenfield, and closely follows an earlier narrative by an Ionian abbot, Bede's brief account should be treated with cautionary respect. Oswald's victory is described in Bede's famed *Ecclesiastical History* as the divinely inspired triumph of a Christian king over a satanic heathen. In fact Cadwallon was baptised, and the enmity between him and the Northumbrian kingdom was intensified by the rivalry between different strands of early British Christianity. As far as Bede was concerned, the Celtic chief was irredeemable, 'an impious man' who deserved an ignominious end. This is hinted at in the account, but given Cadwallon's martial reputation it is just as likely that the Welsh leader was defiant to the end and died in the midst of his slain bodyguard.

Bede exploited the victory at Heavenfield as a eulogy to the princely state of Northumbria and a reinforcement of the cult of the warlike Oswald and his brother northern saints. Despite this, it is highly likely that across these now gentle acres of Northumberland there was once a furious struggle. Although there have been no recent archaeological surveys, for centuries after that decisive day of Northumbrian victory, the battle site gained a reputation for splintered human bone and twisted fragments of sword blades which were turned over by the plough. A field opposite the battle site, to the south of the road, is referred to as 'Moulds Close', well named because of its dark associations with burial and decay:

The place is still pointed out to this day and held in great veneration where Oswald raised the sign of the Holy Cross when about to engage in this battle. Bede, eighth century

As Oswald began to celebrate his great achievement and mourn his fallen comrades, the site of their death became a place of pilgrimage. Monks from the nearby religious settlement of Hexham quickly began to raise a permanent memorial to the day of their salvation. A small chapel may have shared the site with a simple wooden cross, said to have been erected by Oswald as a battle standard before fighting began. His crude cross was soon whittled away by pilgrims greedy for relics and miraculous cures, but it has been replaced over the centuries by a succession of others. One stands there today, carved at now only by wind and rain, but still proudly facing out across the Northumbrian battle line.

By destroying the Welsh invasion at Heavenfield, Oswald had saved his homeland, which prospered briefly until he too died in a storm of slashing blades and piercing arrows. A tiny church dedicated to Oswald now occupies the field of his greatest and most unexpected victory. It is modest yet inspiring. Perhaps it shares something with the plain Christian symbol that he was said to have used successfully as a call to arms so long ago. Beyond question, at any rate, Heavenfield is a seductive place for modern pilgrim and military historian alike.

Oswald's short reign gave a breathing space which encouraged a cultural and religious flowering to take hold in Northumbria. Its apogee is expressed in the beautiful Gospel illustrations produced at Lindisfarne, and the priory church in Hexham, which was famed as a wonder of the Western world after it was built in 680. Northumbria's kingdom vividly illuminated a darkened age until it reeled

Heavenfield's battle cross. Successor to countless others since AD 635.

under a deadly sword thrust from across the grey Northern Sea.

Longboats adorned with distinctive dragon-shaped prows nosed through the sea mist as the Norsemen arrived to give battle. These unwelcome visitors well earned their reputation as 'the great host of heathen men'. But the initial raids on the north-east coast were in fact carried out by relatively small parties of warriors. They attacked with lightning speed and ferocity, inflicting an ancient blitzkrieg on their ill-prepared victims.

In the closing decade of the eighth century, Viking raiders struck first at the Northumbrian monasteries which stood alone and exposed along the extended north-eastern shoreline. Religious colonies at Lindisfarne and Tynemouth were looted and destroyed before any local defence force could be mustered. As the flames rose behind them, the Vikings set sail for their Scandinavian homes but then prepared for further invasions of northern England.

Their earlier attacks may have served well as reconnaissance probes, and consequently at the beginning of the ninth century they returned in greater numbers and began to force their way inland. On this occasion, however, there was a more concerted effort to resist them, even though the power of an independent Northumbria, weakened by internal conflict, was rapidly slipping away and was ended by the large-scale Danish landings into Britain which

> *The pagans from the northern regions came with a naval force to Britain like stinging hornets and spread on all sides like fearful wolves.*
> Simeon of Durham, twelfth century

began in 865. Barely more than half a century later, the Northumbrian kingdom had shrunk back from its original huge area towards the recognisable borders of modern-day Northumberland and Durham. Yet Northumbria could still field a fighting force to be reckoned with and was able to mount significant campaigns against remorseless Viking incursions.

Several large battles were fought against the Vikings, but unfortunately the evidence to pinpoint their exact location is insubstantial and often contradictory. About 833, for example, after landing at Lindisfarne, a large Viking force moved far inland to clash with an English army on the banks of the Tweed close to Carham. During heavy fighting, traditionally held to have taken place in a now anonymous field on the outskirts of the small hamlet, several English counts and bishops were scythed down by the long-shafted Viking battleaxes. On his tour through the North in the early sixteenth century, the antiquarian John Leland seized on this version for his famous history, preferring it to the Anglo-Saxon Chronicle which champions Carhampton in Somerset as the true battle site. Yet it is highly plausible that this area of Northumbria would have been an attractive Viking target. Other local traditions suggest that the Vikings launched vicious onslaughts in the same area, against the Anglo-Saxon administrative and communication centres at Corbridge and the royal 'vill' at Whittingham. After their elimination, the fertile vales surrounding them would then have been at the mercy of the Viking invader. However accurate such a scenario may be, it is certainly true that legends persist of blood-red Northumberland rivers choked with the corpses of battle, as the northern counties marched on into a new millennium of turbulent history.

Although it contained pockets of Danish settlement, Northumbria by the

> *He was a Northumbrian of a hard fighting clan*
> *The son of Edgeleave,*
> *Ashferth his name;*
> *Wavered not at the war play,*
> *but, while he might,*
> *Shot steadily from his sheath of arrows,*
> *Striking a shield there, or shearing into a man,*
> *And every once in a while wounding wryly.* Anglo-Saxon Battle Poem, tenth century

Tynemouth Priory, burial place of St Oswin and King Osred of Northumbria, was destroyed by the Vikings in AD 875.

The monastic community of St Paul's at Jarrow was another target for the Norsemen.

Lindisfarne: Holy Island of Northumbria and cradle of English Christianity. Danish raiders obliterated the first monastic buildings, and the distant ruins are of the post-Conquest Priory Church.

beginning of the eleventh century had become in effect an Anglo-Saxon earldom. And then in 1006, with a poisonous foretaste of interminable strife to come, a Scottish army splashed across the River Tweed. Scotland, too, was beginning to test its growing strength and was led by a ruler, Malcolm II, who was keen to expand his borders and exploit the perceived weakness of his Northumbrian neighbour. The optimism of Malcolm's initial foray ended in his defeat, however, within tantalising reach of the town of Durham and the treasures of the religious community which had not long been established there. Yet the Scottish king's territorial ambitions were not to be denied and he returned eight years later to comprehensively defeat a Northumbrian force. Once again the clash of arms is thought to have taken place near Carham, but again this is far from certain.

Nevertheless, it is generally agreed that this battle served to draw a line of contention along the Tweed and set the port of Berwick in the eye of a storm which raged for centuries to come. But England and its northernmost counties had first to withstand a greater upheaval, as across the Channel, in his capital at Rouen, Duke William of Normandy swore revenge against the oath-breaking English king who had deceived him.

Chapter 2

THE NORTH IN REVOLT
1066–1093

*Preparing therefore a large fleet, he invaded England with nine
hundred ships, and in a severe pitched battle, Harold fell in fight,
and William the Conqueror obtained the kingdom.*
Simeon of Durham, twelfth century

As darkness fell on late afternoon of 14 October 1066, the 'fighting man of Wessex' and his brothers lay dead and barely recognisable on Senlac ridge. The demise of Harold Godwinson and his dynasty brought to a premature end what may well have been a golden age of Anglo-Saxon rule in England, but the survivors of Hastings had no time for the luxury of nostalgia and were faced only with the bitter reality of death or submission. After the battle, the victorious Duke of Normandy paused at his camp before beginning the pacification of the south-eastern counties. Shocked and demoralised by the loss of their formidable war leader King Harold, most of them surrendered without a struggle, and on Christmas Day 1066 William was anointed as the monarch of all England. A few months later, evidently satisfied with his progress, the new king then returned for a short time to his ancestral lands in Normandy. But not all of England was prepared to be subdued without further conflict and in the Conqueror's absence rose in revolt. Although this rebellion ultimately failed to pose a united challenge to Norman rule, Northumbria played a large part in it and was to pay an even larger price for its intransigence.

In the immediate aftermath of William's accession, however, life probably changed imperceptibly for the inhabitants of the North. After their mauling at the Battle of Fulford in September 1066, Northumbria did not contribute fighting men to the Anglo-Saxon levies at Hastings. Labourers continued to toil in the rich pasture-lands around Durham, working busily in the fields but bitterly mindful no doubt of the Scottish raiders who had burnt their crops just a few decades earlier. Yet a chain of tragic events had begun which brought into their midst Norman men-at-arms led by mail-clad knights on their war horses.

Concerned predominantly with mopping up resistance in the southern and western part of his new kingdom, William's initial policy towards the most northern counties was simply to sell off their potentially lucrative control. But this proved at best to be unwise and at worst cynically callous as distrusted outsiders became the new Earls of Northumbria. Even before the Conquest, resentment was brewing in the North against what was regarded as unjust taxation imposed on them by a distant Anglo-Saxon authority. Consequently, if their strongly felt sense of custom and tradition was offended enough, the insular Northumbrians were quite ready to unsheathe their weapons. Also, their separate identity was strengthened by the growing prestige of the community of St Cuthbert. After centuries of nomadic wanderings around the North, this band of monks had settled at Durham from where miraculous fables of the northern saint's preserved body began to spread across the Christian world. Obviously then, the appointment of a non-Northumbrian as Bishop of Durham in 1042, followed by a succession of unpopular earls up to the eve of Conquest, had caused further restlessness of which William either knew or cared nothing. It was no surprise, therefore, when the identity of William's first earl became known, that Northumbria again slid down the precipice towards open rebellion.

In March 1067, Copsig, a Yorkshire noble, became Earl of Northumbria. He followed in the footsteps of the reviled Tostig, who was brother to King Harold but whose only success appears to have been to unite the forces of resistance within Northumbria. From his power base in York, Tostig's overbearing stewardship had brought widespread revolt to the region. Incredibly, William demonstrated utter indifference to this by later preferring Copsig, rather than a Northumbrian rival, to become earl. Copsig had been deputy to the loathed Tostig. There was barely time for an inaugural ceremony. Copsig's only welcome was the thrust of Northumbrian lance.

> William granted the earldom of Osulf to Copsi, who was on the side of earl Tosti, ... Osulf, driven by Copsi from the earldom, concealed himself in the woods, in hunger and want, till at last having gathered some associates whom the same need had brought together, he surrounded Copsi. Simeon of Durham, twelfth century

After only weeks in power, Copsig blundered into an ambush while 'feasting' at Newburn, about five miles west of Newcastle, and desperately sought sanctuary in the nearby church. Although an isolated riverside village, Newburn always had military significance for its fords over the River Tyne. Roman troops are believed to have waded across here, and fragments of stone in the riverside church of St Michael and All Angels may date from that time. Its squat tower overlooking waterside meadows is aggressively Norman, but tucked into its fabric are identifiable traces from the Anglo-Saxon period.

In 1067, the brief reign of Northumbrian Earl Copsig was brutally ended at the Newburn church of St Michael and All Angels.

So it is conceivable that a desperate Copsig may have fled here, pursued by a phalanx of enraged and well-armed Northumbrians. At last they had a symbol of their disaffection within striking distance and they did not consider the implications of their actions. They ignored any plea for mercy and set fire to the building, driving out the hapless earl, whose brief rule ended in a hacking welter of sword and spear blades. While the exact details of this assassination may have been conflated with a later murderous incident where rough justice was similarly meted out to a despised figure of authority, Copsig's brutal removal from power clearly indicates the deeply felt grievance of the people of Northumberland and Durham at a perilous moment in their history.

But William's grip on England was not yet strong enough to retaliate immediately for the loss of Copsig. Not until 1069 did Durham at last fall under the avenging shadow of the Conqueror. From his new castle at York he ordered an expedition to silence the troublesome North forever.

In the piercing cold of January 1069, a large detachment of Norman knights and infantry approached the gates of Durham. Their cavalry contingent may have numbered around seven hundred, one-third of William's estimated attacking force of knights at Hastings. Commanded by Robert de Comines, a Norman Count who relished his promotion to earl, the taskforce had contemptuously ignored a stark warning from Egelwin, Bishop of Durham, not to enter the county. Undaunted and no doubt heartened by the ring of steel surrounding him, Comines rode through Durham's abandoned streets and commandeered its rough collection of ill-assorted houses.

> *In the third year of his reign, King William sent Earl Robert, surname Cumin, to the Northumbrians on the north side of the Tyne. But they all united in one feeling not to submit to a foreign lord.*
> Simeon of Durham, twelfth century

On a peninsula caught by a serpentine loop of the River Wear, Durham provides a sublime position for defence. After crossing the river and entering the town, the Norman column would slowly ascend a steep hillside to the plateau on which a gleaming new cathedral had been built as a repository for Cuthbert's relics. It had been completed in 1017, and probably because of the brilliance of its untarnished stonework, was known as the 'White Church'. Looking out from here, across the darkening valleys and moors, Comines must have felt unassailable as his forces bedded down for the night. At dawn he intended to strike out, perhaps using Durham as a command centre from which to extinguish resistance in the surrounding region.

Even though thick woodland around the church and the inhabited area had been partially cleared, enough remained to conceal all movement in the surrounding valleys. Signals quickly passed around the area calling together a grimly determined Northumbrian assault force. Their approach muffled by the heavy foliage, they quietly assembled and waited to attack. Just before dawn they darted forward, stealthily eliminating sentries and then bursting into streets many of them would have known well. Even before a call to arms could be given, Normans were struck down and the narrow lanes of Durham echoed to the cries of sudden death.

The Norman military machine was a well-equipped, razor-edged battering ram. Their cavalry capability was evolving to act most effectively in open spaces where the speed and power of galloping attacks could pulverise disorganised opponents into the earth. But when taken by surprise in the dark and cramped environment of an early medieval township, the Norman knights and their men-at-arms would hardly be able to lift their sword arms, let alone swing their massive broadswords to any cutting effect.

> *The affair was conducted with great ferocity, the soldiers being killed in the houses and the streets.* Simeon of Durham, twelfth century

Norman soldiers probably died in confused, milling groups in the lower part of the town, as with terrible efficiency the men of Northumbria stabbed and slashed their way to the top of the hill and its command post where Comines was desperately trying to rally his depleted troops. From the roof of the headquarters, placed in ecclesiastical lodgings near the cathedral, a group of surviving Norman spear and bow men desperately kept their besiegers at bay. Raging flames ended their short-lived defence, however, and the building was soon a blackened ruin containing the charred corpse of the Conqueror's failed lieutenant in the North.

Throughout the history of conflict, well-organised and highly motivated combatants waging guerrilla warfare on their native soil have inflicted humiliating defeats on an apparently superior enemy. Hardly twenty-four hours after they had entered Durham, Comines' spearhead force lay dead on its streets. A lone survivor was permitted to struggle back with news of this disaster which had engulfed the Norman army. They had obviously underestimated the ferocity of the enemy ranged against them and were unable to match the Northumbrian fighting men in close-quarter combat. Perhaps if the unlucky King Harold had been able to employ similar tactics, the course of English history would have been changed.

Not surprisingly, the relative ease of the Northumbrian victory emboldened resistance in the North. A firestorm of rebellion spread to the garrison at York where its commander suffered a similar ghastly end as his brother knight Comines.

William's reaction was predictably harsh. He set in motion the notorious 'harrying of the North', a scorched earth policy which at this stage, because of further Danish incursions along the Ouse, was concentrated in the Yorkshire area. Unrest in Cheshire also delayed retribution, and some districts around the Tyne and to its north were consequently spared from the most severe destruction.

Instead, to strengthen his tightening grip on power, William intensified his castle-building programme. Uncompromising fortresses soon towered above town and countryside, constantly visible symbols of the irrepressible Norman occupation. At Durham, in the wake of the Comines debacle, work began on a timber motte which was quickly reinforced by stone. It was raised on a mound opposite the cathedral, maintaining both a respectful distance and a

Durham Castle, high on its glacial mound, was built in 1072, after Robert de Comines and his Norman force were annihilated in the town.

sense of superiority as it watched over Durham and the revered sanctuary of Cuthbert.

The haste in which the castle was built sharply reflected the parlous state of security in the region. William had persisted in transferring authority to unpopular contenders who appeared able enough to calm a belligerent Northumbria. But in May 1080, the weakness of this policy was again made clear to him. On the banks of the River Tyne, with fire and the blood of a bishop, the Northumbrians gave another scornful response to Norman rule:

> *Walcher, bishop of Durham, a native of Lorraine, was slain, on Thursday, the second of the ides of May at a place called Goteshead (that is the goat's head) by the Northumbrians.* Simeon of Durham, twelfth century

It was no surprise that Walcher, the Bishop of Durham, was unwelcome in his new community. After all, he had been appointed in 1071 following the ejection of the Northumbrian Ethelwine. Inflaming local resentment further, the unfortunate Ethelwine was imprisoned by the Conqueror and died in custody shortly afterwards. Subsequently, under a pall of gloom and distrust, Walcher was enthroned as the first Norman Bishop of Durham and became custodian of the new fortress which guarded the peninsula.

Walcher of Lorraine was not a close ally of King William, but his ecclesiastical reputation was outstanding and he was equally renowned for his dignity and political awareness. It seems certain that he made an attempt to reconcile the men of Durham with their new masters but this was at an inopportune time when the sore of dissent was too inflamed to heal. Indeed, tension was only worsened by William's momentous decision uniquely to combine church and state within Durham by selling the earldom to Walcher. From humble origins as a clerk in Lorraine, Walcher had risen to become Durham's first Prince Bishop.

The heady attractions of such high office may have robbed Walcher of his former political astuteness. As earl he rekindled the blaze of earlier unrest by imposing another deeply resented tax upon the region. Similarly, he failed to prevent a further spate of Scottish raids deep into Durham. But above all, in addition to this expanding catalogue of woes, he then became fatally embroiled in the blood feuds of the Northumbrian aristocracy. And so, 14 May 1080 became a day of nemesis for Walcher and the fractious Northumbria he was struggling to control:

> *When the time came, they met at the appointed place; but as the bishop would not hold the meeting in the open air he went with his clergy and more worshipful knights into the church there.* Simeon of Durham, twelfth century

A truce was agreed and Walcher agreed to meet a Northumbrian delegation on the Tyne riverside close to the settlement at Gateshead. It was a surprising decision perhaps, given the bitterness between rival factions and the proximity of the peace conference, in the rebel heartland, to the scene of Earl Copsig's slaughter thirteen years earlier. A small monastery at Gateshead had overlooked the river crossing since the seventh century, and although the exact site is now lost, it probably lay slightly east of the present church of St Mary.

Walcher's attempts at conciliation were ignored and on a pre-determined battle cry, the angry Northumbrians drew their concealed weapons and forced the bishop and his bodyguard back into the church. Wishing to prevent further bloodshed he then bravely faced the levelled swords of his antagonists. His reign, begun in hope and ended in acrimony, was over. So virulent was the animosity against him and the regime he represented, that the Northumbrian perpetrators of this atrocity were prepared to violate the sanctity of a religious

Gateshead St Mary's, close to the place of Bishop Walcher's assassination in 1080.

institution, an uncomfortable prospect in an age of strong spiritual conformity. Shortly afterwards acrid smoke from the burning church drifted over Walcher's mutilated body.

Yet the spear-thrust which killed Walcher also dealt a mortal blow to any lingering aspirations of Northumbrian freedom. On a bare river mudbank known afterwards as 'Lawless Close', a party of monks discovered the discarded corpse of their bishop. Even as they ferried him downriver for burial, a Northumbrian assault battered against Durham Castle, now impregnable on its rocky heights. There would be no repeat of the earlier Norman catastrophe, however. Probably because they lacked the heavier

After its discovery, the corpse of Walcher is believed to have been conveyed to the monastery at Jarrow.

Durham Castle's keep, built by Bishop Flambard about 1100 and rebuilt by Salvin in 1840 to accommodate students instead of soldiers.

equipment necessary to break down a modern fortification, the siege failed and the Northumbrians trudged back to their homes after four fruitless days. Never again were they able to mount a concentrated onslaught against the Norman army of occupation.

William's rage would not be difficult to imagine. Any possible inclination towards compassion had vanished in the flames of Walcher's funeral pyre. To weaken the potential Northumbrian threat he had already forced a sullen oath of fealty from Malcolm III of Scotland. Now there could be no interference as Northumberland and Durham stood alone and exposed, defying King William to the last.

Yet on this occasion, the Conqueror did not cross the Tees to personally chastise his obdurate Northumbrian subjects. Perhaps the legend that he was overwhelmed by superstitious foreboding as he approached Durham Cathedral during an earlier visit has some truth. Instead, Odo, Bishop of Bayeux, who was more amply protected by the spiritual armour of his exalted office, was despatched to wreak the monarch's vengeance upon the North.

Odo was half-brother to William and rode towards the shield wall at Hastings brandishing an iron war mace, but nothing is known of how well he acquitted himself in the actual fray. But he was undoubtedly efficient in his cruel suppression of the remaining resistance movement within Northumbria. Given free reign he appears to have completed the 'harrying' with zeal. Simeon, 'monk and precentor', who is known to have been at Durham cathedral in 1104, has described the effect of the whirlwind of devastation

Spirit and Sword of Northumbria: the Prince Bishop's Cathedral in Durham.

which engulfed Northumberland and Durham during those desperate times. It is written with the graphic outrage of a man who must have been an eyewitness to those traumatic events.

> *It was horrific to behold human corpses decaying in the houses, in the streets, and the roads, swarming with worms, while they were consuming in corruption with an abominable stench. For no one was left to bury them in earth, all being cut off by the sword or by famine. Meanwhile, the land being thus deprived of any one to cultivate it for nine years, an extensive solitude prevailed all around. There was no village inhabited between York and Durham; they became lurking places to wild beasts and robbers, and were a great dread to travellers.* Simeon of Durham, twelfth century

It has even been suggested that significant members of the region's ruling class were summarily executed in a purge intended to end Northumbria's illusions of political separateness forever. Yet no matter how savagely they were punished, the Northumbrians' spirit of distinctiveness would not be suppressed and proved its worth in the centuries of conflicts to come.

Chapter 3

NORTHUMBERLAND BESIEGED

1093–1097

Meanwhile, in the month of May, Malcolm, king of Scots, invaded Northumbria with a large army intending to push on further if he met with success, and to throw his force upon the inhabitants of England.
Simeon of Durham, twelfth century

A s the two northern counties fitfully resigned themselves to foreign domination, a more familiar enemy approached. In 1093, six years after the death of the Conqueror, his old adversary Malcolm III marched south once more. Some have mistakenly said this pugnacious old campaigner was known as 'great head', more in reference to a disproportioned skull than kingship or deep intellectual capability. But his persistence and military opportunism were not in doubt and always figured strongly in dealings with his southern neighbours.

During William's occupation of England, the Scottish monarch was sensibly reluctant to risk a full-blooded confrontation with the Norman army, preferring instead to dart into Northumberland and Durham, raiding when he was certain the Conqueror's attention was elsewhere. A formal peace treaty had been concluded as early as 1072 which had been backed up by further grudging assurances of obedience from Malcolm, but it was soon obvious that he would never fully conform to these. Nor would he completely relinquish his pretensions to exercise a sizeable share of control in the North. In the preceding turbulent years of Northumbrian history, disaffected members of the northern aristocracy had bought safe exile at the Scottish court with nebulous promises that Malcolm and his heirs would inherit the Northumbrian earldom.

Furthermore, in an act of wily statesmanship, Malcolm had strengthened his tenuous northern claim by marriage to Margaret, sister to Edgar Aetheling, an Anglo-Saxon claimant to the English crown.

And so on 11 August 1093, Malcolm III stood in the town of Durham, its gates thrown open to him at last. He was there not as a marauder but as an invited guest. In peace, he came to take part in the foundation ceremony for the vast Norman cathedral which was to soar above the peninsula and obliterate every trace of its Saxon predecessor. It would have been surprising therefore if the veteran Scottish king was not seized by the historic portent of the solemn ceremony which followed. At the birth of this great ecclesiastical building Malcolm was witnessing the consolidation of Norman power in England and a declaration that the North would not be easily prised from its grasp.

After leaving Durham, Malcolm travelled to Gloucester in another futile attempt to make a binding peace agreement. If the Scottish king had any doubt about his future course of action it was resolved by the consequent brusque meeting with a callow William Rufus, son and successor of the Conqueror. Now recovering from some of the problems which had marred his accession, England's new king felt secure enough to treat the tiresome Scottish demands with disdain.

> *On the day of the feast of St Bartholemew, Malcolm, king of Scots, met William the younger.* Simeon of Durham, twelfth century

Malcolm stormed away. In his seventieth year he was an old man who probably now more than ever thought of his political destiny and the brief time left to fulfil it.

Still seething, the Scottish king responded to this treatment in the time-honoured manner. For the fifth and last time, Malcolm III of Scotland bit deeply into the territory of Northumberland. In November 1093, his army laid siege to Alnwick on the banks of the River Aln. Accompanied by his son, Malcolm had begun a campaign which may have been intended to be not just the basic pursuit of 'booty' suggested by some modern historians, but a deliberate attempt to stake a lasting claim to the coveted Northumbrian prize. There were no spoils of war or glorious conquest for the Scots, however, in a disastrous expedition which caused only grief and the mysterious death of their king:

> *He invaded Northumbria with as large an army as he could collect, intending to bring upon it utter desolation.* Simeon of Durham, twelfth century

> *And then it happened that where he had deprived many of life, property and liberty, there he himself lost at the same time his life and his possessions, by the judgement of God.* Simeon of Durham, twelfth century

Although its curtain walls were not to be completed for another half-century, in 1093 the motte and bailey castle at Alnwick was a crucial link in the chain of Norman defences which stretched vertically through Northumberland and Durham, protecting major river crossings and significant townships on the Tweed, Aln, Tyne and Wear. Fortifications here were begun in the reign of the Conqueror and were vigorously continued over the following centuries.

In the medieval period, before the advent of cannon fire, these buildings played a key role in the strategy of warfare. They were built at naturally strong, judiciously selected locations, and often overlaid existing sites. Within the security of their extensive compounds, soldiers could be mustered and equipped not only to man the castle defences but also to mount patrols in the surrounding region. The castle was thus a fulcrum of defence in hostile territory which could also be turned into a springboard of attack. But its static limitations similarly ensured it could be isolated with ease and bypassed if necessary. In such times the surrounding countryside was abandoned to the depredations of the invader until the arrival of a relief force. Usually this was far too late to prevent the looting and gratuitous violence which was customarily inflicted upon any of the local civilian population who had not managed to escape. Despite this, it was difficult for any castle in the path of invasion to be ignored.

During the medieval period, the siege was the common currency of warfare and occurred much more frequently than all-out battle. Once opened, a siege was generally conducted within recognised formalities. If equitable surrender terms were agreed upon, for example, the castle garrison could be allowed to retain their equipment and march out to freedom saluted by the

> *The portcullis assaulted as*
> *you soon may hear*
> *By wonderful daring they*
> *came to the ditches*
> *Those who were inside did*
> *not forget themselves*
> *They soon struck each other*
> *and were mingled together.*
> Jordan Fantosme, twelfth century

fanfares of trumpets. But if the siege had been drawn out or the fighting particularly vicious, the beaten defenders might just as easily be slaughtered like farmyard beasts. Above all, bellowing defiance from the safety of their unbreached castle battlements, a castle's stubborn garrison were always a voluble reminder of failure which honour demanded an invading commander must redress.

The Scottish king may have been in this uncomfortable position on 13 November 1093. It was St Brice's Day and King Malcolm fretted in his camp close to the fortified mound at Alnwick. Not for the last time its formidable defences were able to frustrate a Scottish assault. While its position lacks the towering grandeur of Durham or Bamburgh, Alnwick is guarded by a precipitous ravine on its flanks and the broad River Aln which would impede any Scottish thrust from the north. In the impasse of a situation like this, when a castle could only be starved into submission, it was possible for negotiations on surrender to have been entered into. At Alnwick this may have led to a sudden and dramatic lifting of the siege.

Resting in his tent, Malcolm was alerted to the arrival of an envoy from the besieged castle who wished to surrender and make a symbolic handover of the fortress keys. Jubilantly, the unsuspecting Scottish king advanced to meet him and was then impaled on the lance point of this ambassador of death. The dying king fell and in the ensuing chaos his killer made an audacious escape by plunging into a river teeming with early winter rain from the Cheviot Hills

> *But he was cut off near the*
> *river Alne, with his eldest*
> *son Eadward, whom he had*
> *appointed heir of the*
> *kingdom after him.* Simeon of
> Durham, twelfth century

upstream. Taken by surprise, the confused Scottish forces were then counterattacked by a vengeful local militia under the command of Robert de Mowbray, who had been the Conqueror's final appointment as Earl of Northumbria. Hunters were turned into the hunted as the Scottish besiegers were fatally trapped against river and castle. In the subsequent sharp and bloody clash the Scottish army was driven back, many of them to thrash and drown in the rushing waters of the Aln. Broken and demoralised by the shocking turn of events, the Scottish survivors limped north, leaving the fields and woods around Alnwick littered with the bodies of their dead and dying comrades. Amongst them was the king's eldest son Edward, who desperately fought to avenge the death of his father before he too was mortally wounded by the cleaving English broadswords:

> *The king Malcolm was wounded by Hammund, the constable of the said Eustace de Vesci, with a certain lance, on the point of which he had placed [the key of] the keep of the castle of Alnwick for a pledge.* Chronicle of Alnwick, fourteenth century

These more colourful details of Malcolm's slaying have become established in local folklore which grew from the monkish Chronicle of Alnwick Abbey, compiled well after its foundation in 1147. Clothed in the conventions of chivalric romance, this particular medieval story may conceal a darker truth of treachery and murder at the hands of a common assassin. Similar details concerning the identity of Malcolm's death-dealing visitor can also be regarded as romantic fictions concocted by the Alnwick brethren. They suggest that the killer's name was Hammund, who in recognition of his deadly proficiency was

The Percy Lion, always on guard at Alnwick Castle.

afterwards known as 'Pierce-Eye'. From his descendents were said to emerge the famed Percy family, the feudal northern magnates who came to dominate Alnwick and play a major role in northern history. In fact they accompanied William the Conqueror from Normandy and it is more likely that their name originated in the French town of Percy.

Nevertheless the strength of local tradition cannot be denied and perseveres today at almost every turn in Alnwick's parkland. A short distance from the mighty castle, the river is spanned by Lion Bridge, named for the Lion statue, emblem of the Percys, which stalks along the parapet. Cast in lead with mane and tail flying behind it, the metal Lion stands taut, poised like a powerful arrow shaft, forever pointed at the heart of its enemy in the North. Built in 1773 to the design of John Adam, this bridge is justly renowned as a splendid vantage point for castle views. Less celebrated is a stretch of the Aln below, which recalls a daring swim to freedom. A crossing of the river was once known as

Malcolm's Cross, erected in 1774 to mark the death of the King of Scots at Alnwick in 1093.

'Hammund's Ford'. Further north, major events in the downfall of the Scottish king are commemorated with a stone cross and a boggy patch of ground which was once 'Malcolmswell'.

Regardless of how it came about, the king's death undoubtedly caused a catastrophic reduction in the fighting capabilities of his command. From the earliest days of warfare and through into the Middle Ages, morale continued to depend heavily on the survival in battle of a warrior leader. Malcolm's death disheartened his country as well as his soldiers. Scotland was pitched into virtual civil war over his succession, which at least gave the North a temporary respite from cross-border attacks.

Northumberland did not forget its former Scottish tormentor, however. In death, Malcolm was afforded the respect which an intemperate English monarch had denied him in life. Close by the reputed place of Malcolm's demise, the chantry hospital of St Leonard's was established to offer prayers for the eternal salvation of his soul. All that now remains of the chapel is a skeletal ruin to the north of the castle.

After the battle and before it was reclaimed

Fifteenth-century gatehouse, sole visible remnant of Alnwick Abbey, built in the century following Malcolm's death.

Ruins of St Leonard's Chapel, Alnwick, founded about 1200 for the soul of King Malcolm of Scotland, killed nearby.

for burial in his native land, the body of the Scottish king was borne south. On the headland of Tynemouth, burial place of Northumbria's ancient kings and saints, King Malcolm III of Scotland was laid to rest. This was the last fragment of Northumberland's soil he would ever lay claim to.

Although he was emboldened by his emphatic victory over the Scots, Earl Robert did not allow Northumberland to enjoy a peaceful existence. Like the deceased Scottish king, it appears the Earl of Northumbria did not admire the flame-haired English ruler. From the outset, Robert de Mowbray favoured the elder brother of William Rufus to have a stronger title to the English throne. Consequently, Mowbray was exiled for involvement in a rebellion which tore across the West Country in 1088.

> *Robert de Mowbray, earl of Northumberland, and William de Eu, with many others, plotted to deprive King William of his kingdon and his life.* Simeon of Durham, twelfth century

But in 1092 William II emerged with his crown intact and, displaying a mixture of magnanimity and political realism, he restored Robert to his former northern earldom. In gratitude Mowbray then served his master well, and much of William's confidence in his wayward vassal must have been restored by the spectacular exploits of the earl's army at Alnwick.

Robert de Mowbray had removed a painful Scottish thorn from the side of the English king. Instead of rapprochement between the two men, however, this brought another shudder of rebellion to the North. It was far from the movement of popular resistance seen in the early Conquest, but an ugly squabble between rival Norman factions, which spilled along the coast of Northumberland.

Mowbray maintained a reluctant allegiance to his king until 1095. Then they were irreconcilable. The earl had kept alive his ambition to overthrow Rufus and evidence exists that he increasingly resented what he saw as meddling by the king in the internal affairs of Northumbria. Finally, after a dispute concerning custom duties on the River Tyne, Mowbray was summarily dismissed from his post. By refusing to answer for his actions at the royal court, the wilfully disobedient earl had made a declaration of war. He emphatically did not 'wish to be in the King's peace' as William had requested. His confidence no doubt boosted by his recent success in holding Alnwick, Mowbray then slammed shut the doors of his other major northern fortresses and prepared to resist the will of the English king:

> *For when the matter was known, the king assembled an army from all parts of England, and besieged the castle of the aforesaid Earl Robert.* Simeon of Durham, twelfth century

Newcastle was first to feel the Norman fist. Built by William the Conqueror's elder son Robert in 1080, the original motte and bailey construction may well have been strengthened by Mowbray as he assessed the already strong defensive capabilities of his northern counties after he assumed power. Rearing above the Tyne, the timber walls of this fort controlled the river's first accessible crossing point from the coast. This stretch of river was originally Pons Aelius, a Roman camp and a bridge which supplied it. Before the Conquest it was the monastic township of Monkchester. Now it was becoming known as the New Castle and it became a magnet which drew a powerful Norman strike force towards it.

Determined to make an example of his wayward earl, Rufus rode at the head of his avenging army. He had pardoned Mowbray once but this time the king was determined to cut out the cancer of rebellion that had disfigured his reign. Yet Robert had his escape route well planned and fled east along the river to its coastal tip. At the castle on Tynemouth's craggy promontory, he held his besiegers at bay. With the North Sea at his back and steep cliffs on both flanks, Mowbray grimly endured whilst at the same time making ready for his next flight of freedom.

Knowing he could not face his king alone in open battle had perhaps dictated his puzzling strategy. Trusting the resilience of his northern fortresses, Mowbray may have hoped that Rufus would eventually be forced to bargain while rebellion in other regions fermented in his absence. Evidence from that period suggests that the scheming hand of Mowbray could be detected in a stillborn Welsh plot to unseat the king. But whatever his convoluted motivation, Mowbray had grossly misjudged the determination and patience of King William. Rufus was prepared to leave aside other matters of state until he was certain that the rebellious earl was within his grasp. On first hearing of disquiet amongst his barons, William hinted at his resolution not to buckle under the weight of their demands. William of Malmesbury records a calm and measured statement by the king. It also evokes a chilling reminder that he was the true son of the Conqueror with a sword equally as sharp: 'Only be careful not to upset William the Conqueror's decisions. If they set them aside they should be careful of their own decisions. The same man made them dukes who made him king.'

William backed his rhetoric with brute force. Attacks rained down upon the defences at Tynemouth and the walls tottered but the castle held firm. Mining engineers may have been employed by Rufus to bring down parts of the castle's outer works, and during this operation a squadron of Mowbray's most experienced knights was taken prisoner. Increasingly desperate and starting to behave more like a common fugitive than a Norman grandee, the earl then sought escape once more. His flight from his latest bolthole may have reinforced legendary tales, still current today, of a honeycomb of secret passages which radiate across the surrounding countryside from the depths of Tynemouth Castle. It is more likely that he managed to break out under the cover of a moonless night and slip through the cordon flung around the castle by the English king. Robert de Mowbray, Earl of Northumbria, then covertly moved north along the coastline to his last and greatest redoubt.

Throughout many centuries of continuous military use, Bamburgh was the majestic star of Northumberland's strategic defence. Planted firmly on an iron-hard outcrop of Whin Sill dolerite, soaring 150 feet above the shore, the castle platform dominates the surrounding coastal region. From its walls

Newcastle Keep, part of the great fortification begun in 1080 by Robert Curthose, son of the Conquerer, for 'the Scottes to gaynstande and to defende'.

Tynemouth, refuge for Robert de Mowbray during his ill-fated revolt in 1095.

any garrison could comprehensively survey the neighbouring countryside and hone their weapons to razor sharpness as an enemy laboured towards them.

When he reached Bamburgh, however, William Rufus was prepared for a lengthy stay. The king was well versed in protracted sieges. At Rochester, shortly after he came to power, the castle garrison began to die of starvation before it surrendered to him unconditionally. To tighten the noose around the beleaguered defenders at Bamburgh, the English king ordered the construction of a mighty siege engine, the infamous 'Malvoisin'. A tall tower or belfry which was steadily built up to face the walls of Bamburgh Castle was indeed a 'malevolent neighbour'.

After this he fortified a castle before Bebbanbyrig, that is, Queen Bebba's city, to which the earl had fled.
Simeon of Durham, twelfth century

'Malvoisin' may also have been used as a generic term to describe these siege towers, some of which could be over 50 feet high. When complete, the construction would overlook castle battlements and protect crossbowmen as they wound their weapons before firing down upon the besieged castle. Sometimes these remarkable accomplishments in carpentry were mobile and had to be manhandled awkwardly into place against a castle's outer walls. Hides were draped around the sides of the tower for protection and assaults could be launched from internal staging platforms. Bamburgh's particular wooden persecutor appears to have been of the fixed type, however, erected just beyond bowshot. Manned constantly, it stood as a mocking reminder to the weakening garrison opposite that their supply line was now cut off. Content that his objective was effectively accomplished, Rufus and his escort rode south, leaving the unfortunate occupants of Bamburgh Castle to Malvoisin and malnutrition.

But Mowbray's instinct for personal salvation was undiminished and, astonishingly, he evaded his captors once again. Some sources indicate that the earl was lured out by false promises of asylum at Newcastle, although he spent his final days of freedom back at Tynemouth before he was wounded and taken prisoner.

Bamburgh Castle, Northumbria's most formidable coastal fortress.

Manacled like a common criminal, the deposed earl was dragged in disgrace back to Bamburgh, which continued to hold out under the command of his wife. She was left with no choice by the very real threat of her husband being publicly blinded. Still intact, the great fortress was handed over and Mowbray was led into captivity. After the revolt his fellow conspirator, the Count de Eu, was defeated in trial by combat and barbarously mutilated. For his part, the once mighty Earl of Northumbria was imprisoned for twenty years before, as suggested by some evidence, being released to eke out his final days in the care of the Church. Robert de Mowbray was defeated and shamed while his splendid northern castles stood firm and well prepared to withstand further attacks.

> *He ordered earl Robert to be taken to Bebbanburg, and his eyes to be put out, unless his wife and his relative Moreal should surrender the castle.* Simeon of Durham, twelfth century

After successfully overcoming this latest challenge to his authority, King William II acted to ensure there would be no recurrence in his strife-torn northern provinces. Shortly after Mowbray's rebellion had been stamped out, William of St Calais, the Norman Bishop of Durham, died. Clutching at the golden opportunity offered by a vacant earldom and bishopric, the king filled neither. A troublesome Northumberland and Durham at last fell under the direct control of the English crown.

For the time being, whilst the special status of Durham's community of St Cuthbert was still acknowledged, there would be no dilution of the royal writ between Tyne and Tees. Norman rule in the North was unbridled and the Scots enemy had been driven back. But traditional Scottish designs on the North were merely in abeyance and emerged refreshed by English political instability in the years to come.

Chapter 4

BISHOPS, CASTLES AND KINGS

1135–1174

By his order the archbishops, bishops, abbots, David king of Scots, and the earls and barons of all England, swore that they would keep their fealty.
Simeon of Durham, twelfth century

Until 1135 the northern counties benefited from the friendship between two kings. Though he was born in Scotland, its future King David I spent a formative decade at the royal court of William Rufus and his successor Henry I. During his sojourn, David was schooled in the tastes, values and bureaucratic structures of Norman England, but just as significantly he appears to have gained the respect of King Henry, who knighted the young Scottish prince. At the death of his patron, however, David, who had become King of Scots in 1124, embraced harsh political reality and turned again to his country's agenda of acquisition in the north of England.

In a twin-pronged thrust through Cumbria and Northumberland during January 1136, he struck vigorously at the most northerly fortresses of Norham and Wark. Both covering River Tweed crossings, these strategically paramount border posts obviously bore the brunt of most Scottish attacks. During clear weather the castles are just visible to each other, but this was probably little consolation for their fatigued watchmen scanning the distant approaches. To the Scots, these were only the first towers of English resistance to be toppled before they could stream onwards to the exposed thoroughfares of invasion.

Within barely a month, much of the North was in David's possession. Of

The Tweed: armies forded this great river and signalled the onset of war.

Once a mainstay of border defence, now barely more than the motte survives of 'Auld Wark upon the Tweed'.

Norham was in possession of the County Palatine of Durham, and from the early twelfth century its castle was the Prince Bishop's major border stronghold.

all the major strongholds, only Bamburgh and Durham did not surrender to him as his substantial army swept southwards. This was obviously a significant Scottish enterprise rather than a speculative raiding foray. The Scottish king had timed his assault to exploit the political chaos which had ensued in England following the death of his former benefactor King Henry. Empress Mathilda, the only heir to the English king, was unacceptable to many of the hierarchy of the Norman state, and the throne was seized by Count Stephen of Boulogne, grandson of William the Conqueror. But he was headstrong and argumentative, having inherited few of his grandfather's qualities of kingship, and Mathilda soon pursued her rightful claim.

At the time of the Scottish king's invasion in 1136, the Norman consolidation of power was well advanced throughout Northumberland. By then over twenty baronies were in place, which deferred to the crown for their privileges. It would not be surprising, therefore, if the teetering loyalty of some northern barons contributed to David's largely unopposed dash through Northumberland. This was a time when the dividing tightrope of political allegiance was particularly difficult to walk, bearing in mind that King David had already sworn support to Mathilda's cause. Indeed, shortly afterwards during the

Certain of the counts of England withdrew their support from King Stephen, and while they were fighting amongst themselves gave certain evil people the opportunity to make mischief, so that the greater part of the kingdom was left desolate.

Simeon of Durham, twelfth century

next Scottish invasion, Eustace Fitz John, who had recently taken possession of Alnwick, one of the richest of all northern estates, openly sided with David and accompanied him on his rampage towards Durham.

Despite these problems with his dissenting ruling class, King Stephen still reacted to the irksome extra threat in the North. He marched to meet David, but to parley not to fight. On 5 February 1136 he bought off the Scottish king by what was to become the first Treaty of Durham. In its terms, David was placated by control of the Cumbrian territory which had always figured prominently in his demands, backed by firm assurances that the coveted Northumbrian earldom would presently be his. However, Stephen's concessions were probably interpreted as an indication of his growing weakness and served only to delay David in his quest to annexe the entire northern region.

Consequently, at the beginning of 1138, in an almost predictable replay of his opening campaign, David returned to the border. His aggressive deployment brought Stephen north again, but battle was avoided by an immediate Scottish withdrawal as David reprised the evasive tactics favoured by his predecessor Malcolm III. Only when the beleaguered English king was drawn away by the deepening crisis in the south did the Scottish king go on the offensive once more. Yet on this occasion he was met with a more spirited show of northern defence. Wark steadfastly resisted David and was left under blockade as the frustrated Scottish besiegers moved off in search of easier prey. Bamburgh maintained its invulnerable reputation, however, and repeated attacks by despairing Scots were flung back from its precipitous walls. So frenzied and merciless did the fighting become that during a sortie on a castle embrasure that was under repair, no quarter was given to a luckless band of captured English defenders. Their dreadful execution, described routinely in contemporary sources as being 'put to the sword', gives only the briefest hint of the savagery which characterised the conduct of both sides during these violent episodes. It was only a foretaste of what was to come during the subsequent brutality of Anglo-Scottish attrition.

Despite the setbacks suffered by the Scots, there was no sign of further English intervention, and by midsummer of 1138 David I of Scotland had once again mastered the North. But his ambitions were not yet

> *The Scots overrun it all like devils.* Jordan Fantsome, twelfth century

satisfied. Although he was largely in control of Northumberland and Durham, his slackly disciplined and disparate force, its ranks thickened with a large foreign contingent, crossed the Tees and moved into the open moorland of north Yorkshire. Near Northallerton in August 1138 the Scottish invaders were resoundingly defeated, not by Stephen who was virtually penned into the South by Mathilda's determined bid to oust him, but by a local army hastily assembled by the Archbishop of York. Fortunate to escape with his life from the bloody rout, David and his son scuttled back across the border at Carlisle to contemplate a future suddenly cast into uncertainty.

Because of his parlous situation, the increasingly insecure Stephen was forced into further humiliating backtracking. To avoid another invasion along a northern front he was not in a position to defend, the English king had to pay a high price. David soon gave warning that he was not a spent force and pressed again at the border, forcing an end to the epic defence of Wark. It was all too much for Stephen. And so it happened that, by means of the second Treaty of Durham in April 1139, David of Scotland was ceded the Northumbrian earldom and finally controlled the northern counties. Ironically, after being brought at last to a major battle in Yorkshire and crushed decisively, the Scottish monarch was quietly handed much of the territory he had campaigned for in the north-east.

Yet, crucially, the lands of St Cuthbert, the historic home of the saint's holy people the 'haliwerfolk', stretching between Tyne and Tees, were set aside from the charter. Durham's great castle was the strategic cornerstone of the region and the King of Scotland, rather than attempting direct military action to seize it, set out to exert control over the bishop who ruled from within its formidable walls. King David's attempt to complete his northern domination through the intervention of his scheming Chancellor began one of the most extraordinary incidents in Durham's long and embattled history.

From an obscure background, William Cumin had climbed to the highest office in the administration of the Scottish monarchy. This Norman former chancery clerk

> *There was a certain Chancellor of the King of Scotland called William Cumin.* Simeon of Durham, twelfth century

at the court of Henry I may have been at Durham on the staff of his patron Geoffrey Rufus, who was appointed bishop there in 1133. But even if he was not present to witness it personally, he must have been aware of the singular combination of secular and temporal power that Durham's Prince Bishops began to dispense during this period. Perhaps the seed of overarching ambition began to grow within Cumin then. But its unseasonable flowering in 1141 brought only anarchy to Durham as armed men stamped through the streets and pushed aside monks in the candlelit aisles of the cathedral itself.

In that year, Bishop Rufus became gravely ill and shortly before his death on 6 May was visited by Scotland's Chancellor. During his episcopate, Rufus had resolutely spurned all Scottish blandishments and remained staunchly loyal to his English king. As the life of the bishop drew to a close, however, David of Scotland embarked upon a patently manipulative policy to extend his authority. It is not clear exactly who hatched the subsequent plan of usurpation but David clearly backed Cumin to succeed Rufus and supported his Chancellor in an incredible plot to conceal the death of the ailing bishop. In effect, a religious coup would take place allowing William Cumin, placeman of the Scottish king, to be installed at Durham.

For an unseemly three days, with the complicity of some of the deceased bishop's staff, his embalmed body was denied burial and his death was unannounced. Without a formal election, Cumin, ringed by a well-armed Scottish contingent and supported by several northern barons who owned extensive Scottish estates, then assumed control of the bishopric.

Strong protests were made in the cathedral, particularly by its prior and archdeacon who stoutly insisted that the process of legal election from an agreed group of suitable candidates be adhered to. These Durham officials bravely asserted the independent canonical rights of their community and emphasised their traditional privileges as the guardians of St Cuthbert, which they earnestly believed even the greatest power would not dare to compromise. Eager to delay this roughshod trampling upon their traditions, the community of Cuthbert then appealed to Rome for papal intervention. Faced with the threat of excommunication but buoyed by pledges from the camp of a resurgent Mathilda, Cumin pressed onward nevertheless. He was determined to have Durham, even if it was threatened with destruction in the taking.

By 1142, although he still retained his grip on the city, Cumin was becoming politically isolated as former allies drifted away and resistance to his rule became bolder. Most fundamentally, his mainstay of support, David of Scotland, began to distance himself noticeably after Stephen of England was released from captivity to rejoin the political fray and again bewilderingly shift the balance of power. As a result, in what must have seemed a bitter slight to Cumin, David proposed an alternative Scottish candidate who would be more acceptable as bishop and calm Durham's escalating tension.

> Enticing some with illicit promises, luring others with flattery, getting round everyone with exquisite astuteness, and doing everything within his means and beyond his means to ensure that the power he had presumed to take on himself should remain in his hands...
>
> Simeon of Durham, twelfth century

But David had underestimated his Chancellor's abiding instinct for aggrandisement. Apparently unabashed, the uncrowned bishop brazenly continued with his misappropriated duties, even using the official seal of the Palatinate for his correspondence. The tangled ecclesiastical arguments on his legal status were rapidly drawing to an end, though. Now William Cumin would increasingly have to depend on the fighting ability of his soldiery to retain his plundered see.

Cumin's interregnum at Durham would have been impossible without the fealty of prominent northern barons. But Roger de Conyers, who held tracts of land across southern Durham and into Yorkshire, had stood out against the Scottish interloper from the start. And in 1143 when the Dean of York, William St Barbe, was unanimously elected to be Bishop of Durham, Conyers moved against the now discredited Cumin.

Twelve miles to the south of Durham city, Bishopton, which had been granted to Conyers by his patron, Bishop Rannulf, now became the focus of resistance to Cumin. With prescient haste, Bishopton was strengthened, drawing the forces of Cumin into an ineffective assault on the motte and bailey fortification. It is easy to appreciate why the attack was such an abject failure, for even after almost a millennium, the site of Conyers' motte and bailey castle retains an air of towering invulnerability. On the fringes of a tiny village, on ground still marshy underfoot, the earthen dome of Bishopton castle rears almost 40 feet upwards like a malevolent distortion in the smooth

Bishopton was a focus of Durham's resistance to William Cumin. It now rivals Elsdon as the best preserved motte and bailey earthwork in Northumbria.

countryside which surrounds it.

Failing to dislodge his principal enemy from Bishopton was a severe blow which had serious implications for the faltering cause of Cumin. Former allies began to desert the erstwhile Chancellor and Bishopton became a rallying point for his disaffected enemies, particularly after the legally appointed bishop, William St Barbe, arrived there in the summer of 1143. In a great show of strength, Conyers and his companion barons then escorted St Barbe to Durham from where they were resolved finally to eject the Scottish impostor.

A base was established at the Church of St Giles, elevated on a riverside bluff to the east of the city. From the churchyard, Conyers and his men were beyond arrow range and well placed to appreciate the defensive strength of Durham:

> *Its steep and precipitous appearance warns off the enemy, it also despises hostile hands because of the encompassing river. Neither battering ram nor ballista can be employed against it.* Lawrence, Prior of Durham, twelfth century

After the envoys despatched to treat with the garrison were greeted with arrows and abuse, Conyer's troops could not have relished the prospect of storming the legendary citadel which confronted them and St Barbe may have been similarly haunted by the loss of life and damage to castle and cathedral which would inevitably follow. But Durham and the shrine of Cuthbert remained intact.

As battle approached, the confidence of William Cumin, both in the solidity of his castle walls and his inexhaustible fund of stratagems, did not

The area around St Giles in Durham was commandeered as an observation post during the struggle to oust Cumin from the bishopric in 1143.

waver. Financial inducement appears to have been the most dependable weapon in Cumin's strategic armoury and it certainly seemed to quicken the pace of Count Alan as he marched to the rescue from Richmond. The arrival of this bribed recruit at Durham persuaded St Barbe to scale down the tension. St Barbe seems to have been much more of a bishop than a prince, sharing few of the tendencies of his more bellicose successors. His may have been the deciding influence which then resulted in a controlled withdrawal to Bishopton during which Conyer's rearguard was harried at each step by the ascendant forces of Cumin who 'cruelly slaughtered as many of the rear ranks as they could capture.'

During their prolonged encampment in Durham, his men had never been renowned for their discipline, but increasingly Cumin appeared to unleash them from any semblance of control. They roamed at will and torched St Giles and Kepier Hospital on the outskirts of the city. Even the cathedral was not spared from their orgy of vandalism. With undisguised disgust, medieval chroniclers relate how the hallowed precincts of their church were turned into a barracks by loutish soldiers who prevented the clerics from fulfilling their daily offices. Durham was sliding into a morass and Cumin was the Lord of Misrule who presided over it:

> *There you might have seen soldiers in their armour, with drawn swords in their hands, running up and down between the altars; archers, some intermingled with weeping and praying monks, others brandishing swords over their heads.* Simeon of Durham, twelfth century

As 1143 drew to its close, in an attempt to end this pandemonium, the coalition opposing Cumin built a new fortification at Thornley to the east of Durham city. This may have encouraged Cumin to enter into a short-lived truce, which was ended as he struck out again across the county to punish those barons who had not kept faith with the pretender in Durham cathedral.

But in 1144, with a perversity born of medieval *realpolitik*, Scottish intervention helped to close this chaotic chapter as effectively as it had begun. From the island of Lindisfarne, far from the battle front, the ultra-cautious St Barbe opened negotiations with the Scottish monarchy. Henry, heir to the Scottish throne and Earl of Northumbria, at last weighed in on the side of legality, promising to uphold William St Barbe's claim. By mid-August, the scene was set for a final confrontation.

Yet with his usual foresight, the cunning Chancellor had already arranged a truce with Earl Henry, and as the deadline approached his soldiers began to fortify the church at Kirk Merrington, barely six miles from the city walls. The square outline of Merrington's church of St John the Evangelist projects starkly from a high limestone ridge. In the valley far below it, the River Wear curls eastwards towards Durham city and even today St John's appears to be as much castle as church. When it was rebuilt and extended in the nineteenth century, much of the ancient design was retained, especially its landmark tower. The obvious defensive potential of the church was seized upon by Cumin's men who furiously dug emplacements around it. Although softened by the growth of centuries, a low rampart to the north of the churchyard remains as evidence of their efforts.

But the soldiers' labour was in vain as the barons of Durham who opposed Cumin exacted their pent up fury against his henchmen. In what seems to have been a surprise attack, a force led into combat by the northern triumvirate of De Conyers, Geoffrey Escoland and Bertram de Bulmer smashed against the fortified church.

If the ramparts around the building checked the initial assault, it is probable that the hard-pressed defenders could not hold the open ground for long, forcing a knot of Cumin's men to pull back from the shattered remnants of their dead or demoralised comrades and make a forlorn last stand in the church behind them:

> *They shot arrows and hurled darts at all who came within their reach.* Simeon of Durham, twelfth century

From the relative security of the church interior and tower they maintained

St John the Evangelist, Kirk Merrington. With the defeat of his soldiers here in 1144, William Cumin's grab for power in Durham was dealt a fatal blow.

a steady arrow fire which temporarily suppressed the attack, but Conyers would not be cheated of victory now. Braving the deadly bowshot hail, some of his men stormed forward to hurl 'firebrands' through window openings and bring the vicious action to a blazing conclusion.

It is likely that Cumin remained in Durham during the battle, and if he looked across from its southern walls he would have seen the flame-streaked horizon and grasped its significance immediately. Without the military muscle to enforce his benighted rule, his aspirations for the subjugation of Durham were brought spiralling to earth. Any faint hopes for salvation that he may have harboured were then dashed by King David, who informed him that there would no forthcoming Scottish support.

His grand mission at an end, Cumin embraced the inevitable, yet was probably disingenuous to the last. Pleading forgiveness, and admitting the error of his ways, he left Durham to its rightful bishop, who belatedly occupied the Palatinate throne. With the pious St Barbe at the helm, Durham regained some stability and the apparently contrite William Cumin faded from the historical record. But it was unlikely that the misplaced talent of this artful manipulator would remain untapped. Such devious skills would always enable

> *He repented him of his former evil deeds and humbly offered to make ready satisfaction for all his trespasses.* Simeon of Durham, twelfth century

him to chart a course through the murky waters of medieval political life. Indeed, evidence exists that he did rebuild his administrative and religious career, although becoming an archdeacon in 1157 must have been a poor substitute for the high office that had been prised from his grasp.

To the monks at Durham who catalogued this disruptive period in their history, William Cumin, apart from the obvious handicap of his Scottish connection, was a devil incarnate if not the Antichrist himself. Their lurid accounts of his disreputable conduct, concentrating particularly upon the depraved treatment of his prisoners, have accordingly tended to distort subsequent historical interpretations. It may be injudicious, therefore, to accept wholeheartedly that for example, Cumin 'exercised unheard of cruelties.' Or that throughout his fractious rule, 'The very name of Durham … became a source of terror, and a place formerly consecrated by religious reverence, was feared and deserted as a kind of hell on earth.'

Notwithstanding such self-righteous indignation, there is no doubt that over five disturbed years, life in Durham city was thrown into confusion and the region was pitched into war by the hubris of one man. William Cumin may have begun his nefarious tilt at power as the instrument of the Scottish king, but he also increasingly viewed the bishopric as his own personal fiefdom, to enrich him and to be endowed upon the dynasty which would succeed him. Similarly, in a reign founded on dishonesty, Cumin resorted to every ploy, from forgery to naked aggression, to retain power. But, equally, there is no doubt that there were enough men of Durham brave enough to confound his plans. They fought fiercely to uphold the traditions of their cathedral and keep Durham afloat on a sea of Scottish domination in the North.

Once the fabulous medieval shrine of Cuthbert, Durham Cathedral has become an architectural icon of Northumbria. Modern pilgrims now throng this World Heritage Site.

During the ill-starred reign of King Stephen, the North was largely abandoned to Scottish control. But Stephen's successor, Henry II, was made of sterner stuff. After the death of the combative King David in 1153, the Scottish crown passed into weak and ineffective hands and Henry gathered Northumberland back into the English fold. Many of the Scottish ruling class were shaken by what they regarded as craven deference to their traditional foe and waited for the chance to reap a harvest of revenge.

Twenty years elapsed until the Scottish Lion stalked the fields of Northumberland. William of Scotland had come to the throne in 1165 and was called 'Lion' more in recognition of physical bravery than his political finesse. In 1173, renewed insurgency had damaged the southern political consensus, as the son of Henry II made a bid for the English throne. In return for the support of Scotland, he promised to ratify its territorial claim and thereby unleashed the Scottish host again on the long-suffering North.

> *The hills and the valleys dread his coming.* Jordan Fantsome, twelfth century

William of Scotland's first attempt to storm the bastion of Northumberland came to nothing. Only Warkworth amongst the castles as far south as Newcastle succumbed to him until the threat of chastisement from an approaching English levy forced him back to Roxburgh and a brief truce. His incursion followed a well-rehearsed strategic pattern. After penetrating deeply into Northumberland, the Scots avoided major battle to further their distinct political objectives. Their army remained intact and the North was opened as a second front to draw resources away from the South and complement the disruptive efforts of their rebellious English allies.

In many respects the nature of William's army benefited this relatively fluid approach to war. It had a large component of extremely mobile Galwegians, described vividly by George Tate, the Victorian historian of Alnwick, as 'almost naked but fast moving and lightly armed with small knives and javelins which they could throw at a large distance'. Practised foragers, these fierce tribesmen were adept at surviving on the barest rations and were feared skirmishers. But their wildness also meant that they could be impossible to control, as the Scottish king and the population of Northumberland were shortly to discover. And so, in the early spring of 1174, as the marching ground began to dry out, William opened his campaign plan for the North and the deadly game of war was afoot once more:

> *Then came King William to Wark in England*
> *A castle in the marches which afterwards made him great war*
> *Labour and trouble and often great annoyance.* Jordan Fantsome, twelfth century

After repeating their earlier failure at Wark, the Scottish army raged across the border, trying their luck to the west around Carlisle before resuming the

Prudhoe Castle: besieged but never taken by the Scots. By permission of English Heritage

Warkworth Castle still dominates the village from every angle.

race towards the south. With Flemish mercenaries at its densely packed core, the Scots expeditionary force continued to beat a destructive path through Northumberland until they came in sight of the Tyne and, on a steep riverside cliff, its guardian castle at Prudhoe. With Odinel de Umfraville in command, the castle keep delayed the Scots long enough, allowing the consistently tardy English relief to muster. Honour temporarily satisfied, but Prudhoe still standing, King William then pulled his army back as English armour rattled towards it from its base in Yorkshire. But the Scottish infantry did not leave Prudhoe unmarked. A Chronicle relates that before marching away, they wantonly destroyed the apple orchards which then surrounded the castle.

As it contracted homeward, however, the tail of the Scottish army inflicted a venomous sting. Peeling off from the main force, one division, led by the Earl of Duncan, descended upon the small town of Warkworth, which lies in a coil of the River Coquet about three miles inland. There they vigorously set about the castle and the town which clings tightly to its feet.

> *Knights and sergeants and the other foragers*
> *Take and destroy the land next the sea.*
> Jordan Fantsome, twelfth century

Although of obvious strategic merit, it seems that on this occasion, the magnificent Warkworth Castle was hardly an obstacle to Scottish progress. On his earlier dash through Northumberland, William of Scotland 'did not deign to stop there, so weak was the castle, the wall and the trench.' It is conceivable that few repairs had been carried out by July 1174 when Warkworth was overrun for the second time.

Spoiling for a fight, the raiders turned their attention instead to the church of St Lawrence. Cowering within its thick walls was the local population, hoping to escape the wrath of the Scots who began to burn the village. But the Northumbrians of Warkworth did not survive this day of infamy as, without compassion and without regard to age or sex, they were killed by the invaders. Incensed, the English chroniclers of the atrocity were, perhaps excusably, prone to even greater than usual exaggeration. Some numbered the dead to be over 300, yet beyond doubt the slaughter of innocent civilians on that grim day was fearfully great.

Probably rebuilt in the immediate decades after 1174, the riverside church of St Lawrence is one of the finest examples of Norman architecture in the

Warkworth: begun by the son of a Scottish king in 1139, it was Percy influence and power during the late fourteenth century which completed this outstanding castle.

One of Northumberland's largest and finest Norman churches, Warkworth's St Lawrence was a scene of tragedy on 13 July 1174.

region, a place where peace and dignity can be seen to have overcome hideous cruelty. Yet this wonderful building also serves as a salutary reminder of the everlasting sorrow and pity of war.

But, indirectly, William of Scotland was also harmed by the barbarity of his countrymen. Waiting for his army to regroup, he prepared to lay siege to Alnwick with the remaining column. But he had not reckoned on the anger and initiative of the northern barons who remained unmolested behind the Scottish lines:

> *Good valiant people,*
> *four hundred knights with their shining helmets,*
> *They will be in the battle with him.* Jordan Fantosme, twelfth century

Resolved not to let the Scots escape unpunished, the barons launched an audacious operation utilising local intelligence to assess the deployment of Scottish troops around Alnwick. In the pale twilight before a summer dawn, the gates of Newcastle disgorged a phalanx of several hundred horsemen who struck out northwards.

Apart from his sword and armour, a good warhorse was every Norman knight's most prized possession. Bred for aggression, the battle stallion was trained to run unswervingly at a target, galloping at full tilt. Accordingly, the northern shock troops which bore down upon Alnwick were likely to have covered the thirty miles steadily, conserving their mounts for a decisive charge.

Fortunately for the Norman cavalry, their arrival may have been masked by fog which wreathed about the castle. As it cleared, William of Scotland, who had also risen early and was taking an early morning canter, was horrified to recognise the fluttering pennants and emblazoned surcoats of his enemy as they spurred towards him. Although he was only lightly escorted and may not even have been fully armed, the 'brave, wonderful and old' Scottish monarch faced the onrushing forest of lances. He did not flinch, but in the clashing throng and bone-splintering collision of mounted combat which followed, he was immediately

> *Many a gentle knight has since lost his life,*
> *Many a good man has been unhorsed, many a saddle emptied,*
> *Many a good buckler pierced, many a breast plate broken.*
> Jordan Fantsome, twelfth century

unhorsed and taken prisoner without a struggle. Sparing his shame, some accounts insist that his horse was run through, but it is similarly possible that the dashing King of Scots was literally brought crashing to earth by an error of horsemanship at a crucial instant. William was bundled away and although his depleted corps at Alnwick then appears to have mounted a brief rally, they were cut to pieces by the Northumbrian cavalry. The remaining Scottish

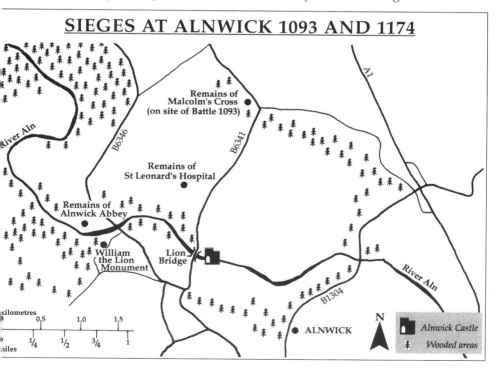

SIEGES AT ALNWICK 1093 AND 1174

Remains of Malcolm's Cross (on site of Battle 1093)

River Aln

B6346

B6341

A1

Remains of St Leonard's Hospital

Remains of Alnwick Abbey

William the Lion Monument

Lion Bridge

B1304

River Aln

kilometres
0.5   1.0   1.5

miles
¼   ½   ¾   1

N

ALNWICK

Alnwick Castle

Wooded areas

Hidden at the entrance to Alnwick's Hulne Park, a Victorian monument, replacing a grander predecessor, recalls the downfall of William the Lion of Scotland at this spot in 1174.

columns, with uncanny similarities to their collapse at Alnwick in the previous century, when they were also violently shorn of a charismatic leader, melted back across the border with barely a murmur.

With a lightning strike, the northern troopers had scored a startling victory. Chance may have played an important role in their success, but there is no doubt that their dawn manoeuvre was brilliantly planned and executed. At the same time, the Scottish leader was guilty of an irretrievable combination of military blunders. Complacently, the Scots monarch had divided his command and turned his back on an underestimated enemy whose castles he had failed to reduce. Now the Scottish king and his country would suffer far-reaching consequences of this ignoble defeat.

Taken from the keep at Newcastle, the humbled King of Scots was stripped of the spurs which were a symbol of his knighthood and ignominiously led to Richmond on a lowly palfrey, his feet bound under its belly. Later, kneeling in homage at the feet of Henry II, the Scots king effectively delivered his country into the hands of England. Overlordship of major forts in southern Scotland was humiliatingly relinquished, as well as Berwick, which reverted to English control. William's age-old hope of recovering the Northumbrian earldom was also dashed. To celebrate the downfall of the Scottish king, church bells pealed across the North. William the Lion had been tamed but his country would not be subdued so easily.

Chapter 5

ANVIL OF BATTLE
1215–1333

Scottish attempts to salvage their fondly imagined northern birthright stuttered hesitantly on through the early decades of the thirteenth century. William the Lion was restored to his throne but died confused and embittered and no closer to the Northumbrian earldom. His successors similarly failed to secure a permanent hold on the North, although for a brief period the army of Alexander II reprised the grim Scottish play, driving southwards to wedge open the cracks of England's creaking political edifice. And then, almost unexpectedly, peace was declared. Recognising both the short-lived cohesiveness of an English state led by Henry III, and his own dissent-riven country, Alexander II of Scotland consented to the Treaty of York in 1237. Historic claims to the earldom were given up and only Tynedale and isolated Northumberland manors were retained by the Scottish crown. Over half a century of relative calm settled onto the mauled borderland. Fields were tilled without interruption, livestock was fattened and barns began to fill with crops. But perhaps inevitably in this violent age, war came again to haunt the North. This time its cause could be laid at an English door.

On his huge black charger, Edward I, the fearsome warrior king of England, rode North to imperial conquest. His querulous Welsh provinces were ringed by a stone wall of English castles and Scotland was now to be subdued. During the protracted squabble over Scottish succession following the accidental death of Alexander III in March 1286, Edward had maintained a dignified restraint. In 1296, however, his patience exhausted and the border unsettled once more, he marched to exercise what he considered to be his rightful but hitherto neglected sovereignty over Scotland.

Newcastle was thronged with the northern levy as they prepared to snatch Berwick from Scottish hands. It was taken back with the utmost ferocity. The iron-capped English footmen scythed down Berwick's wretched townsfolk without compassion until ordered to stop by Edward himself. With a clash and spark of steel which would resonate through Northumberland, 'Longshanks' had struck the first cruel blow in a titanic Anglo-Scottish war.

> *The Englishmen came not onlie with a mighty power by land, but also with a great navie by sea towards the said towne of Berwicke.* Ralph Holinshed, sixteenth century

King Edward's matchless talent to weld together sword and state made him one of the most powerful and feared leaders in the medieval age. Once decided, his military plans were acted on without delay or compromise. Within six months of Berwick being retaken, Scotland was prostrate at Edward's feet, the Scottish army was broken and the Stone of Destiny was *en route* for Westminster. But this English 'hammer' of the Scots had also unwittingly planted the flower of Scottish unity. It was nurtured by William Wallace and Robert Bruce and the North would suffer when it bloomed to maturity.

'Braveheart' Wallace sped south to hack at Northumberland with his great double-handed sword in the icy winter of 1297. After his startling decimation of the English army at Stirling Bridge on 11 September, the North lay open to full-blown Scottish retribution. In the wake of the shocking English defeat, John de Warenne, who commanded the English forces in Edward's absence, was ordered to stand firm until reinforcement arrived. But shadowed by Wallace, the blustering old campaigner Warenne retired instead towards Berwick, before backing away into Yorkshire with the chastened remnant of the English expeditionary force. What remained of Berwick was promptly reoccupied by the Scots but they could only glare impotently at the defenders of its castle who gestured their contempt. Wallace led a lightly armed force largely drawn from the 'lesser folk', as few of the Scottish gentry wholeheartedly supported him. The Scots barons were self-serving, obligated to the English monarch, or sneeringly dismissive of Wallace's comparatively humble origins. Nevertheless, the fierce loyalty of the Scotsmen who did flock to the banner of Sir William Wallace more than compensated for what they lacked in armour or sophisticated siege equipment. But without these they could have little effect on Northumberland's rocky defensive core.

From London, calls were issued for the mobilisation of a northern defence force, but this could not even get under way until December. Not for the first time or the last, Northumberland and Durham stood unprotected as they anxiously anticipated the scourge of Scottish retaliation.

Meanwhile the Northumbrians put in hand preparations for self-defence. Newcastle town became a refugee camp as byways and tracks became congested with civilians rushing headlong towards the South. Royal castles on their way would not make them welcome unless they could pay the requisite entrance fees demanded by the castellans, but Newcastle, even though its walls were not complete, accepted the swelling additional populace and began contingencies for imminent hostilities.

Continuous watch was kept around the town boundary and the inhabitants worked feverishly, demolishing any outer buildings which might impede a clear line of fire from the walls. As to be expected, though, defence of the town was concentrated upon the castle, where almost two hundred archers and crossbowmen were gathered. In the darkening days of late autumn they might have made their weapons ready and jostled for the best sniping positions on the castle ramparts.

Scottish infiltration into north Northumberland began in October 1297. Mounted on their hardy ponies, the tough Scots fighters moved stealthily into the forest area around Rothbury at the centre of the county. From their woodland hideaway they could then strike out with virtual impunity across Northumberland's rolled out patchwork of fields and secluded vales. Skirting major castles, they fell upon undefended towns and hamlets, firebrands ready to hand. Felton Mill,

> *That same year, William Wallace with his army wintered in England, from Hallowmas to Christmas.* John Fordun, fifteenth century

Yeavering and Akeld were amongst the gazetteer of Scottish arson, yet it seems this was merely a precursor to a more concerted attack with Wallace at its head.

But his destructive orgy did not go unchallenged. Northumberland's castle garrisons, most notably from Alnwick, sallied out to divert the Scots from some of Northumberland's more valuable strategic assets. This may have occurred at Newcastle, for Wallace did not attack the town but swung west along the Tyne, smashing Bywell and Corbridge before clattering up the riverside slope into Hexham priory church at the beginning of November. Here he paused for breath and, affording the historic priory some respect, did not burn it but held it to ransom instead.

Corbridge escaped the unwelcome attention of neither William Wallace nor Robert Bruce on their onslaughts through Northumbria.

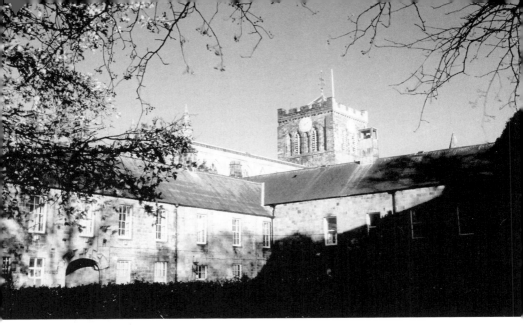

Hexham Priory paid dearly to be spared by Wallace in 1297.

Although heavily damaged by a Scottish wrecking spree in the previous year, St Andrew's Priory in Hexham was left relatively unscathed on this visitation, but Wallace must have been considerably richer when he arrived in Carlisle. Then, with the flamboyance of all bold military leaders, Wallace pivoted his thrust of attack and returned to Northumberland. Reinforcing his army with the Galwegian bands who had been wreaking chaos in central Northumberland, William Wallace plunged south through the Tynedale corridor, wrongfooting his dazed enemy as he squeezed what booty remained from the weary North.

In worsening weather he billeted again with the long-suffering Augustinian monks of Hexham, before turning eastwards along the Tyne towards Newcastle, which stood to arms once more. Speculation persists about the ultimate strategy of Wallace at this crucial juncture. Chroniclers contend that he contemplated an extension of his campaign across the Tyne into the bishop's domain, but was dissuaded by foul weather and concerns about the strength of a local force mustering to oppose him. But the Scots might have relished a meeting with Anthony Bek, the Bishop of Durham. The resplendently noble Bek was a true Prince Bishop, spending as much time on horseback as in the cloister. He was a key political aide of Edward I and was closely associated with the surrender and public humiliation of the Scottish king, John Balliol. Bek was left to fight another day, however, and cast off his mitre for coif and helmet in the defeat of Wallace at Falkirk in the summer of 1298.

Newcastle was left untested too; although the riverside vill of Wylam did not escape and some brazen Scots were provoked to swim the swirling Tyne.

They survived with enough energy to vandalise Ryton on its southern bank. According to the Chronicles, shocked locals scurried southwards bellowing the familiar tiding 'The Scots are coming', but on this occasion the wild followers of Wallace did not. The River Tyne marked the limit of Wallace's excursion as he finally bent northwards into the teeth of a blizzard, overrunning the fortifications at Mitford, possibly scorching the walls of its church of St Mary Magdalene with a fiery trail which the keen eye can detect to this day.

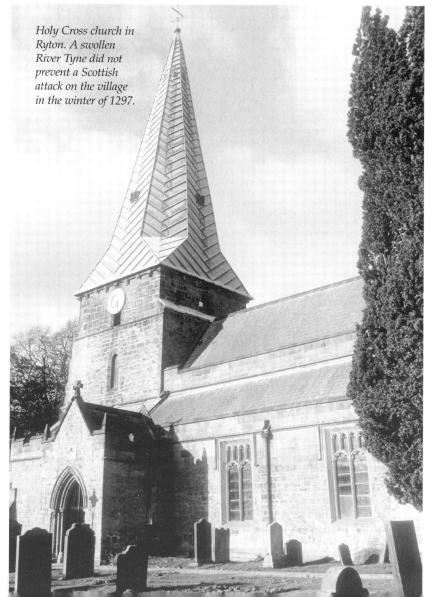

Holy Cross church in Ryton. A swollen River Tyne did not prevent a Scottish attack on the village in the winter of 1297.

Built about 1150, Mitford Castle was steadily weakened by a stream of Scottish invasion until its final destruction in 1318.

Mitford's Romanesque church of St Mary Magdalene still bears the scars of Scottish fire and sword.

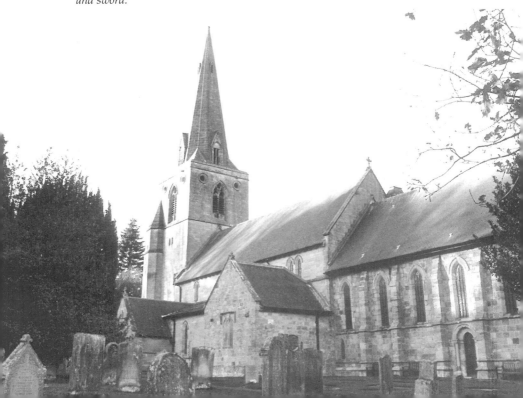

Pious commentators of that time believed that Wallace was driven away by a divinely inspired snowstorm. But it was more likely that an invasion begun as an exuberant backlash against a vulnerable North after the English army had been flayed at Stirling, had run its natural course. As his armies trailed back after him across the border, the Scottish leader may even have sensed some relief. England's strength was reviving and soon Berwick was back in its hands. Wallace's troops

> *Having burnt up the whole land of Allerdale, and carried off some plunder, he and his men went back safe and sound.*
> John Fordun, fifteenth century

were famously capricious, and he admitted that for much of the time he could not control their excesses. At least now they could be regrouped in Scotland to fight and die for him during his final blood-soaked struggle for freedom.

In life, 'Braveheart' was never to revisit Northumberland. But after his brutal execution and dismemberment in London's Smithfield, his once-feared sword arm and shoulder haunch were gruesomely displayed on the twelve-arched bridge leading to Newcastle. Before the withered skeleton fell into the middens below, it was said the arm of the great warrior turned and slowly lifted. It pointed north to his homeland and victory at Bannockburn.

A successor to Roman and medieval river crossings, Newcastle's Swing Bridge (foreground), opened in 1876, now points the way to castle and cathedral.

Sir William Wallace's glorious but brief resistance to English domination paved the way for the triumph of Robert the Bruce. Scottish independence was won in the bloody maelstrom of Bannockburn in 1314 and the North would now be forced to pay for the preceding years of Plantagenet aggression. Old but still magisterial, King Edward had died while on campaign, but was succeeded by a weak and ineffectual son. Edward II could not break the formations of Scottish spearmen during the epic two-day battle at Bannockburn and was equally unsuccessful in preventing the Scottish plunder of the North which followed.

Like Wallace before him, Robert I of Scotland pounced upon the northern counties. To this new Scottish king, the North continued to be the traditional recipient of Scots retaliation and a fattened milch cow to supplement the economy of his straitened country. But unlike those of Wallace, the raids of Robert Bruce, which intensified with almost monotonous regularity after 1314, were conducted in a more systematic and indeed almost orderly fashion. Bruce's campaign was also much more extensive, combing through Northumberland and Durham to include Yorkshire on his itinerary of extortion. Embedded in this strategy lay a primary political objective. With Machiavellian ruthlessness, Bruce was determined to force recognition of his legitimacy as the fully fledged monarch of an irrevocably independent Scotland.

> *The bishoprike of Duresme all throughout Northumberland he brent with hoste full stout.* John Hardyng, fourteenth century

To achieve this, his raids into Northumberland and Durham were short, sharp and regular. And, until 1327 they proved to be extremely lucrative for the Scottish exchequer. Money was their primary objective, rather than other more bulky assets, difficult to transport. But if ransom was not given over promptly enough, fire would surely follow.

Between 1311 and 1327, no fewer than eight separate visits were made to Durham by Bruce's marauders, and even the Scottish chronicler Fordun expressed guilt that Cuthbert's citadel was severely damaged by fire in 1312. Yet this was insignificant in comparison to the material destruction wrought on Northumberland during this dire era. The financial clout of the bishopric and its relatively sophisticated administrative structure often allowed it to buy off the Scottish fire-raisers. Payment of this medieval version of 'Danegeld' was, however, largely beyond the means of its neighbouring northern county.

> *The Scots entered the northern parts of England with a strong hand on 15 June, and wasted it with fire and sword.* John Fordun, fifteenth century

As a result, Northumberland was harrowingly punished and many of its people were driven from the charred stubble of their land, never to return. Even nature then conspired against the despairing population. Not only were they forced to contend with the asset-stripping Scots, but they were also victims of widespread famine after virulent disease had swept through their livestock herds. Yet evidence has also emerged to indicate the resilience of these rural communities. Despite their litany of misfortune, large numbers of their inhabitants returned to the plough to begin a tentative recovery.

History now regards Robert the Bruce and William Wallace as being from the same mould. With some justification, these two Scottish warriors are lionised as valiant freedom fighters, heroically struggling to throw off the English yoke. But to the medieval people of Northumberland and Durham, Bruce and Wallace were only two more apocalyptic horsemen from the North: parasitic Scots invaders who dislocated and destroyed lives which were precarious enough in ordinary circumstances.

Prayers must have been earnestly offered up for delivery from these seemingly incessant Scottish raids. Yet there were signs of a revival in English military prestige. There stirred a renaissance of hope for the North and it was carried into County Durham on the regal shoulders of a boy.

The miserable reign of Edward II was ended by his forced abdication and imprisonment. In July 1327, at fifteen years of age, his son was sent north to earn his spurs. Responding to the latest Scottish assault on the North, this time led by Bruce's trusted Lieutenant Sir James Douglas, a combined force of English levies and mercenaries moved to block the enemy's escape route at Newcastle. With the youthful Edward III as its nominal head, the new English regime controlled by Queen Isabella and Roger Mortimer was demonstrating that disunity was in the past for England now, and further Scottish freebooting would not go unchecked.

But the English campaign was hamstrung from the start. Incessant rain ruined the food supplies of the English and sapped their morale. Flemish mercenaries and English archers fought each other instead of the Scots who, unsurprisingly given their numerical inferiority, continually refused to be drawn into a major battle. The contrast between the two armies could not have been greater as the lightweight Scottish clansmen darted across the narrow valleys and tangled moorland of south-west Durham, pursued by the heavily armoured English, laboriously dragging a baggage train which may even have been weighed down by primitive artillery pieces. Famed Scottish ability to survive on meagre rations was described by Jean le Bel, who served with the English during the campaign:

> *Under the flap of his saddle each man had a broad plate of metal; and behind each saddle a little bag of oatmeal, so that when occasion needed cakes were made of oatmeal and baked upon the plates; for the most part however they ate the half soddened flesh of the cattle they captured and drank water.* Jean le Bel, fourteenth century

Guided only by smoke from burning homesteads, the English trailed behind the Scots until they were eventually located in the area of Stanhope. English spirits may have lifted at last as the young king was led along the lines of his bare-headed soldiers, rallying them to fight and warning them that to ignore the word of command could result in their execution.

But preparations for battle were premature. The Scots again flouted the chivalric convention and ignored Edward's request to fight at an agreed time and place. Instead, with typical boldness, Lord Douglas staged a night attack on the English camp. His lightning assault was checked, but it came within yards of Edward's tent and may have been intended to snatch the young king for ransom. With the armies separated by the River Wear and the Scots occupying the most advantageous ground, a tense standoff was broken in the dead of night by Scottish action. This time, however, they slipped from their parkland camp and sped away, leaving the slaughtered carcasses of the bishop's cattle to mock the efforts of their exasperated English adversaries.

Edward's debut campaign had ended in relative failure and adolescent tears. But the Scots had fled and were back to their shieling homes across the border within three days. The rigours of Weardale must also have shown the boy king how far was the messy reality of warfare from the troubadour's mythical song. His first great army disbanded, the disappointed royal youth left the North. When he returned, Edward III was given the battle that had eluded him.

Failure to defeat the Scots in 1327 was politically expensive for England. The purse strings of the English exchequer would not be stretched further to finance more border protection and Robert Bruce's continued threat to Northumberland forced England to the negotiating table. Soon to become termed the 'shameful peace', the resulting treaty led to a coup which beheaded Roger Mortimer and left Edward King of England in reality as well as name.

Now unbridled, Edward repudiated his earlier recognition of an independent Scottish monarchy and donned his grandfather's mantle of feudal supremacy over the Scots. At first covertly, the young king backed a caucus of disgruntled Scottish knights who sought to retrieve their dispossessed estates. Sailing from England, a force of these 'disinherited' men landed in Fife to roundly defeat a Scottish army at Dupplin Moor. Stung by their defeat, the Scottish backlash was aimed predictably towards Northumberland and vigorously responded to by the newly empowered English monarch.

On 19 July 1333, Edward peered out from his vantage point on the northern slope of Halidon Hill. Below him the coastal plain gradually fell away to the broad River Tweed and the smouldering buildings of Berwick two miles to the south-east. Almost as a routine opening to Anglo-Scottish hostilities, Berwick Castle had again come under siege. Since 1318 the battle-torn town had been in Scots hands, but the death of Robert the Bruce in 1329 brought the border cauldron to the boil again.

> *Behind them a fine town defended by warlike men, on the right a wide deep sea, on the left hand a hollow of the River Tweed which the rising tide fills to the margin of its banks.* Canon of Bridlington, fourteenth century

King Edward appears to have relished the prospect of a renewed war with the Scots. No doubt he smarted at the thought of his humbling by them in Weardale. Now in his adulthood, the English king was free to lead his own campaign and prove his worth on the field of battle.

Berwick, for centuries in a bloody tug-of-war.

Stepping down to the Tweed, the 'white wall', built in 1297, only hints at the long-lost magnificence of Berwick Castle.

His opportunity galloped towards him in the form of Edward Balliol, King of Scots, who owed his crown to Edward's support. Balliol scrambled across the border, barely evading Sir Archibald Douglas and other supporters of Robert Bruce who were not prepared to let the dream of Scottish independence die. They were prepared to give their lives to restore it, and the borderland around Berwick would be the anvil on which their hopes were hammered out.

During the early fourteenth century, Berwick had grown in strategic importance for England and Scotland alike. Apart from its significance as a sea port and the considerable custom revenue it could generate, the town stood out as a major fortification on the north-east coast after Robert Bruce had razed other large castles throughout southern Scotland. Possession of Berwick was therefore regarded as the key to victory in Anglo-Scottish war and Balliol was sworn to return the battle-scarred coastal town to his English patrons.

With renewed support from the English king, Balliol's assault force arrived outside the crenellated towers and walls of Berwick in March of 1333, pledging never to leave them until they were in Edward's keeping. Berwick stood ready to receive the attack. Walls had been repaired and the castle, which was separate from the town, had been garrisoned with seasoned troops. Undeterred, Balliol's men set up camp and began to isolate the town and cut off its water supply.

Led by Sir Archibald Douglas, 'Guardian of Scotland', Berwick's relief force was not far away. But confident in its defences, Douglas at first swerved away from the town and moved into Northumberland to draw off the besiegers. Needing no better excuse than defence of the realm, Edward launched wholeheartedly into open war.

In preparation for the approaching conflict, Edward moved his court to the North and arrived in Durham on 8 April, accompanied by his queen, Phillipa. In what must have been a climate of growing urgency, the men of Durham between sixteen and sixty years of age were then called upon to defend their territory. Newcastle was to be the point of mustering six weeks afterwards, timed to coincide with the docking of a naval fleet in the River Tyne. Berwick was to be given respite from neither land nor sea as the military build-up continued apace.

King Edward seems to have shared his grandfather's enthusiasm for the machinery of war, and two stone-hurling catapults made from the timber of forty oaks were built to order for the campaign. Chronicle accounts suggest that early forms of artillery were also got ready. They were transported directly by sea to complement the arsenal soon to be unleashed upon

The king gathered a great power and besieged Berwicke.
John Stowe, sixteenth century

Berwick. Nothing seems to have been overlooked as Edward prepared to take a town and through Balliol to control a country as well.

By the time the English king arrived to take command at the mouth of the Tweed two months later, Berwick already must have already shown considerable evidence of its pounding by the forces of Balliol. Its walls were blackened and its buildings cracked open by English siege engines and cannons. Their fusillades were described by the English Chronicles of Brut to have 'destroide meny a fair hous and churches also were beten adoune unto the erthe, with gret stones spitouse comying out of gonnes.' So great was the damage that over a year later parliamentary petitions were still being received for compensation.

Bombardment on land was backed by a seaborne assault. High tides in the medieval period allowed ships to sail up to Berwick's walls and on 27 June an attempt was made to land English soldiers onto its accessible ramparts. Anticipating this attack, the Scottish defenders met it with a firestorm of tar-soaked brushwood. Disastrously for them, however, it did not engulf the ships but was fanned back into the town, worsening the already severe damage.

To enable the hard-pressed defenders of Berwick to damp down the flames, a truce was arranged. Hostages were given over and a timetable of surrender was agreed to by Edward, who must then have sensed that the town was almost his.

But then Berwick's yearned for rescue approached. Douglas returned with an army to match the English. Early in the morning of 11 July, as the time for Berwick's surrender drew nearer, massed formations of Scottish troops forded the Tweed. They emerged on its southern bank, slightly downstream from Berwick but apparently unseen by English eyes. Moving further east they came to within striking distance of the besieged town and halted. They drew no closer, content instead with burning the village at Tweedmouth and probing the English defensive ring. Anchored English ships were attacked and Scottish cavalry punched their way through to the town's crumbling old bridge. Some even managed to penetrate the town's outer precincts before they were confronted by an English contingent of knights led by Sir William Montague. In a spirited counterattack he had galloped along the edge of Berwick's eastern shore to pitch many of the surprised Scottish infiltrators into the swirling waters of the Tweed estuary.

Thwarted by the sharp English response to his relief attempt, Douglas resumed his diversionary tack. In an increasingly desperate attempt to loosen the English stranglehold on Berwick, the Scottish Guardian dragged his army southwards to raid into Northumberland and threaten Bamburgh. King Edward was unmoved. Even the presence in the coastal fortress of his queen could not dent his iron resolve. Displaying a ruthlessness that would have been appreciated by his grandfather, Edward instead proceeded to hang his most important Scottish hostage, Thomas Seton, son of Berwick's warden. Seton's body dangled from a tall gallows for all of Berwick to see and consider. Cruel as this was, his action belonged to the same bizarre convention of medieval war which saw Edward granting safe conduct to women and priests or sending his doctor to tend noble prisoners.

A scenario not unlike Bannockburn, where siege led to battle, was unfolding at Berwick. Embraced in a medieval *danse macabre*, the combatants agreed to a final surrender of the town if it was not relieved by 20 July. Confrontation loomed as the truce drew inexorably towards expiry.

After the failure of his feint towards Bamburgh, Archibald Douglas was left with little realistic option but to return and face Edward's comparatively well-rested troops. Leaving about 700 men to guard against any surprise attack from within the town, the young English king moved his main force the short distance north-west to his chosen site of battle.

Thus on the morning of 19 July Edward began deploying his men on the 500 foot high slopes of Halidon Hill, and thirteen miles to the west, from the parkland around Duns, the great army of the Scottish Guardian began its fateful march.

Attempting to mask his approach, Douglas moved in a wide arc, in the shadow of a slightly higher ridge to the north of Halidon. But his manoeuvre was discovered by English scouts, who galloped back to Edward with news of the nearing Scottish host. At about midday their vanguard was sighted by Edward's army which, like the Scots, was deployed into the usual trinity of battle order. Scottish evasion was at an end in the North and the frisson of impending battle must have chilled the summer air.

As he had done as a boy in Weardale, Edward addressed his three divisions

A gathering storm over Berwick, seen from Halidon Hill.

from horseback. But on Halidon Hill, the king then dismounted to join his men-at-arms in the central rank. Following a cavalry disaster at Bannockburn and the clumsiness of the Weardale campaign, the English way of war had begun to change. Consequently, by 1333 much of Edward's army rode to the battlefield then fought on foot. Furthermore, from about the time of Edward I, the longbow played an increasingly significant part in English warfare. Although the Welsh are widely credited with its introduction, many English archers were equally adept in the skilful handling of this lethal battle-winner and English bowmen of the shires were undoubtedly well represented in Edward's army drawn up on Halidon Hill. They were prominently arrayed, possibly in projecting horns from Edward's three battle divisions or the harrow-shaped formations mentioned in the Chronicles of Jean Froissart.

> *The English who were sitting on their horses watched the enemy advance to battle, whereupon they sent away their horses and in a light step took their places in the divisions.* Canon of Bridlington, fourteenth century

Flags unfurled, the Scots drew nearer. Beginning their descent from the crest of a hill known as the 'Witches Knowe', the Scottish knights dismounted. Like the English, they joined their comrades on foot and their horses were led back to be tethered behind the lines. But unlike the English, it was a tactic the Scots would bitterly regret.

The dismounted men-at-arms fell into step with the schiltrons, the traditional massed bodies of Scottish footmen. They advanced steadily, their spears a jagged forest against the midsummer sky. Moving further into position, they paused to witness a challenge by a giant Scotsman named Turnbull, which was taken up by Robert Benhale, an English knight. By all

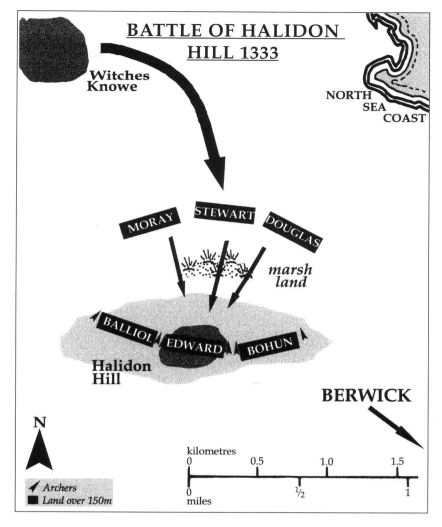

BATTLE OF HALIDON HILL 1333

accounts the resulting duel was brief and the schiltrons pressed forward, past the decapitated corpse of their fallen champion. After this symbolic defeat, a more tangible misfortune awaited the Scots.

Before they could ascend the slope of Halidon to close with the English front rank, the Scottish formations were forced to traverse a band of marshy terrain. Much of it has been drained long ago, but the former condition of this land is more than hinted at by 'Bogend', the name given to the modern farmstead which occupies the site. It became a muddy graveyard for many Scots footsoldiers who struggled across it in 1333.

Halidon: crest of the hill and front line for the army of Edward III in 1333.

Halidon: a view towards the north-west, area of the Scots' arrow-torn approach to battle.

Any momentum built up by the schiltrons was now lost and as they finally began to labour up to the waiting English battle line they came within range of its waiting bowmen at about two hundred yards. Hundreds of bowstrings were drawn back and bodkin-tipped volleys hissed through the air. Careful aiming by the English longbowmen would hardly have been necessary. The most proficient amongst them was able to loose up to twenty arrows per minute. Unchallenged, they poured their 'clothyard' shafts into the Scottish formations spread invitingly across the slope below them.

> *They could bear neither the storm of arrows or the weapons of the knights.* Canon of Bridlington, fourteenth century

Their elevated angle of fire would have given the goose-feathered missiles extra impetus as they plunged into their slowly moving human targets. Legislation required the Scottish footman to equip himself with a bascinet, a cloth-padded covering for his upper torso, and protective gloves. These would have afforded some measure of protection but virtually any high-velocity arrow strike into vulnerable soft tissue, if not fatal, could disable a combatant. At the least a sustained longbow attack could bring widespread disruption to cavalry and infantry ranks alike.

Yet according to a chronicler's description of the battle on Halidon Hill, the Scottish army came forward on foot with heads bent into an arrow storm which was 'as thik as motes on the sonne beme'. On an incline appropriately named Heavyside, fell the greatest number of Scottish dead. Despite this, and urged on by their commander the Earl of Moray, the survivors made contact with the English front. Ironically, the division on the English left led by Edward Balliol appears to have taken the weight of this Scottish attack. Balliol would now have to risk all to reclaim his briefly held Scottish crown.

But their prolonged advance over difficult terrain and under withering bowshot had sapped the Scottish fighting strength. And their ordeal by arrowshot was not yet over. During the battle's progression, the English bowmen had been largely undisturbed. The Scottish horses that could have driven them from the field were presumably grazing contentedly on Witches Knowe. Now, the English archery wings may simply have folded back as the Scottish men-at-arms drew within sword length. Expending their remaining arrows, the English bowmen were then given free reign to pepper the Scottish rear ranks, delaying them from supporting their fighting comrades.

Both front lines were now joined into a dreadful melee of armoured men who swung their weapons and stabbed at each other at every opportunity. In the murderous crush where death was as common from suffocation as from sword wounds, the depleted Scots divisions began to falter. Although first to join battle, the Scottish right wing began to give ground, edging backwards from the killing blows of Balliol's comparatively fresh fighting men. It was enough. Retreat by the Scots right wing was a critical setback to the rest of their exhausted and disheartened force. Order amongst the remaining Scottish divisions disappeared as they were overwhelmed by the awareness of impending defeat. The urge for self-preservation became impossible to resist.

A general rout commenced as Scottish fighting units disintegrated into an undisciplined mass which spilled back down the slope of Halidon.

Mounting their horses, the English pursued and quickly overtook their floundering Scottish opponents, striking them down with 'iron-shod maces'. Those fugitives who managed to reach the Witches Knowe ran no further, for they were abandoned by their grooms who sped away on the warhorses that might have saved them and could have turned the battle in their favour.

> *How manliche thai pursuede the Scottis, that flowen for drede. And there might men see meny a Scottissheman caste doun unto the erthe dede, and meny a gode habrigoun of stele in hir blode bathede; and many a time the Scots were gadrede in companies, but euermore thai were descomfitede.* Chronicle of Brut, fifteenth century

Only Hugh, Earl of Ross is recorded to have gallantly stood his ground, pleading with his fleeing countrymen to face the oncoming English horsemen. His corpse was discovered amongst the piles of Scottish dead. In this 'rueful battle', so many of the nobility perished, including their leader Sir Archibald Douglas, that the Scots chronicler Fordun was too distressed to list them. The English chroniclers showed no such restraint, and one of them reckoned the entire Scottish dead to number an implausibly high sixty thousand. Even allowing for the partiality of medieval accounts, there is no doubt that the Scots had suffered a heavy loss of life in their failed attempt to relieve Berwick, while English casualties were remarkably few.

Berwick was English once more and Edward III had made his mark as a great warrior king, exorcising the ghosts of Bannockburn and Weardale. Characteristically, contemporaries ascribed his triumph on the summit of Halidon as much to the hand of God as to man. Yet beyond question it was the English longbow, allowed to shoot without interruption from a strong defensive position, which decisively influenced the outcome of the battle at Halidon Hill. Victory at Halidon was a further vindication of the changing military tactics which the English had initiated at Dupplin Moor in 1332. Some contemporaries thought that on Halidon's grassy slopes, the power of English bowmen had dealt Scotland a mortal blow. But her strength was astonishingly recovered and soon forced English arrows to fly once more.

Chapter 6

RED HILLS AND MOORS
1333–1402

Complete as it was, the English military success at Halidon Hill in 1333 did not guarantee security in the North. English archery may have helped to propel Edward Balliol back to the Scottish throne, but antipathy towards English control and their surrogate king showed no sign of diminishing.

Resistance coalesced first around Sir Andrew Moray, and then, more importantly, around the son of Robert Bruce, David II. He was taken to France by Scots lords fortunate enough to survive the butchery at Halidon, and during an exile which cemented the Franco-Scottish alliance the impressionable adolescent was no doubt continually reminded of his country's suffering at English hands. Returning triumphantly to Scotland in 1341, the ambitious young king was determined to prove himself a worthy successor to Robert Bruce and retraced his father's path of war through northern England. The incursions of 1342 and 1345, which penetrated far into Northumberland and Durham, were the flexing of Scottish military muscle. Soon afterwards David II would return with all his country's might.

In the wake of Halidon, Edward of England had seemed content with nominal control of Scotland. A renascent Scotland steadily prised its land back from the English after 1337, when Edward turned his attention to a more attractive foreign prize. France instead became his cockpit of war, culminating in the extraordinary English victory at Crécy on 26 August 1346. Against the odds, English archers outranged Genoese crossbowmen and deflected successive charges of French cavalry, helping King Edward to a success which eclipsed even Halidon.

Humiliated by the enormous defeat and desperate to save Calais, which Edward was threatening with a reinforced English army, Philip VI of France pleaded with his Scottish ally for assistance. Had the French won at Crécy, David would probably have seized the opportunity to invade with slightly more enthusiasm, yet on 7 October 1346, his schiltrons marched towards the South.

> *That he [Philip VI of France] would make war on England; for he said, he should take on hand on his side to make war too.* Andrew Wyntoun, fifteenth century

With the despatch of a huge English army for the attack on Calais, David thought it was reasonable to assume that defence of the North would be sparse. But Edward was far too competent for such strategic neglect. To counter the potential Scottish threat in the king's absence, plans had been laid as early as March to hold back the levy from north of the Trent. When the call went out, however, despite the patriotic appeal of victory at Crécy, the northern muster generally proceeded with difficulty, hampered by desertions. Nevertheless, a force was assembled in time to oppose the Scots. Its complement indicates what a rich seam of archery skill, established by widespread practice at the target butts, was available to England at this date. It is possible that a third of this reserve English army gathered for homeland defence were bowmen. Most of them were the men of Lancashire and Yorkshire, sufficiently strong of arm to haul back the strings of their six-foot bowstaves. Under the command of the Archbishop of York, the Sheriff of Yorkshire and northern magnates Henry Percy and Ralph Neville, they moved from Richmond to confront the unsuspecting Scots.

David had chosen the western flank of Northumberland for his invasion, but this was not to be the brief campaign of rapid movement favoured by his father Robert Bruce and by William Wallace before him. In the autumn of 1346 David proceeded at an almost processional pace, seeming to anticipate a longer and more comfortable stay. His army, famously inured to hardship, were it seems to be spared their usual privation and he commanded them not to burn major towns in Northumberland and Durham, preserving them as supply centres to ease an anticipated leisurely homeward march. Similarly, the Scottish king and his retinue were not prepared to forgo luxury in the field. Thomas Samson, an English clerk, later reported the Scots to have 'put up their tents and pavilions of the richest and noblest sort, the likes of which had not been seen in these parts for a long time, and they provided themselves with victuals for a long time.'

As well as supporting the French, David II was motivated by the desire for revenge. Shortly after crossing the border his army spent several days attacking the minor fortification at Liddel, near Carlisle. After a forthright defence but inevitable surrender, its keeper Sir Walter Selby, condemned as a turncoat by the Scots, was dragged into his courtyard and killed in front of his two sons, who then suffered the same hideous fate.

Ransom was accepted from Carlisle for its salvation, before Lanercost Priory was severely damaged and Hexham was terrorised for three days. At Newcastle, David thought the bridge too strongly defended and pulled his army westwards to enter the Palatinate by their familiar Tyne fording point at Newburn. Apparently not intimidated by its patron saint's aura of invincibility, the Scottish army then closed in on Durham city itself, which appeared ready to negotiate for its protection. By the evening of 16 October, David of Scotland was quartered in the Prior of Durham's residence at Bearpark close to the River Browney and a bare two miles from the cathedral's central tower. Within the bishop's walled park, the Scottish army rested at their cooking fires. Thomas Hatfield, Bishop of Durham, was at Edward's side in France, but another militant churchman, William Zouche, Archbishop of York and one of the commanders of the English army, was much closer to hand.

Early on the following day, William Douglas, Lord of Liddesdale, leading a large foraging party towards the South, blundered into the English vanguard. They had stayed briefly overnight on the outskirts of Bishop Auckland, within six miles of the Scottish base, and at dawn moved out to surprise the Scottish invaders. Poor weather may have suddenly restricted visibility, but for a distinguished leader such as Douglas to mortally endanger his command in this way, confirms that the Scots still lacked any intelligence on the strength and proximity of their enemy. David of Scotland's army would suffer doubly for this negligence.

After a severe mauling, the Scottish foragers, hotly pursued by English horsemen, fled in disarray to warn the main army. Memories of that tangled pursuit and the heavy casualties inflicted upon the desperate Scots have become etched into the district's folklore. The north road from Thinford to the main crossing of the Wear at Sunderland Bridge must have been strewn with Scottish dead. Their abortive flight is clinically recalled by 'Butchers Race', the local name associated with the killing ground to this day.

> *William then returned to the Scottish army, hot and shouting very vigorously, 'David, rise quickly; look, all the English are attacking us.' David replied that this was not possible, saying, 'There are none in England but wretched monks, disreputable priests, swineherds, cobblers and skinners; they dare not face me.'*
> Lanercost Chronicle, fourteenth century

At Bearpark, on hearing of the English arrival, King David may not have been as sneeringly dismissive as the melodramatic Lanercost Chronicle contends, but he would certainly have known that battle was imminent and ordered his army on to the surrounding moorland and towards Neville's Cross.

Crossgate Moor crowns a long strip of land high above the River Wear and to the west of Durham city. Today the moor is dominated by thunderously noisy crossroads, but on the morning of 17 October 1346, it was ominously silent as the massed ranks of two great medieval armies stared at each other across the coarse grassland of a treeless moor.

Following their stunning first blow during the action at dawn, the English army, many of them on horseback, steadily ascended to the ridge of Crossgate

The Prior of Durham's residence at Bearpark: damaged by the Scots before the Battle of Neville's Cross in 1346 and ruined by them during the Civil War in 1644.

Brancepeth Castle: Neville stronghold in Durham from the early thirteenth century.

Moor from Sunderland Bridge in the valley bottom.

Unchallenged, the English army advanced further down the moor, with the cathedral and its protective river loop on their right, while their commanders sought a likely place for battle. Familiarity with local topography must surely have given the English a distinct advantage here. Brancepeth Castle, held by Ralph Neville, a leader in the English vanguard, was close by. Similarly, many of the foot in the English front line were men from Durham about to fight on their home ground.

> *There the people gathered, on the moor between Durham and Bearpark, around the hour of prime [daybreak].*
> Chronicle of Meaux Abbey, Yorkshire, fourteenth century

From the generally nebulous descriptions, it cannot be known definitively where the opposing armies were deployed before the battle of Neville's Cross on 17 October 1346. Yet even after seven centuries, enough still survives of the landscape of battle to provide a vivid glimpse of that ferocious day.

Crossgate's high ridge has been cut through by a railway, but just to its north there remain deep ravines, pinching in the moor at each edge. Across this axis of defence, the English came to a halt, the tip of their left flank resting on the steep valley now overlooked by Arbour House Farm, and their right amply protected by the even more precipitous slopes of Flass Vale. To their front the platform of moorland narrowed to a funnel into which their enemy could be drawn.

Halidon may have been still fresh in the minds of the English field commanders but Crécy was fresher still. Two months earlier in France, John Neville had witnessed the effectiveness of longbows firing from carefully chosen, well-defended positions. Now he stood with his father at the English front line on Crossgate Moor as the archery divisions filed into place. The Scots, of course, had been taught a more painful lesson by war. Robert Stewart had somehow survived the arrow-borne carnage at Halidon and was among the Scottish left-hand division as it spread across the moor from its encampment. Perhaps his counsel was heard, as the Scots halted and stayed beyond arrow range during this tentative initial phase.

Because of the constricted width of the moor at this point, the English may have deployed bowmen on each side of the central division. Alternatively, a solid band of archers may have been drawn across the entire English front, but this could have hampered the army's ease of movement and is difficult to reconcile with the complex manoeuvring of the subsequent battle.

At the core of the English front, warrior Bishop William Zouche addressed their waiting ranks. He exhorted the kneeling troops to fight and prepared their souls for death as the spears of the schiltrons bristled in the opposite lines.

> *And while they arraying were,*
> *The English archers came so near,*
> *That shoot among them well might they.*
> Andrew Wyntoun, fifteenth century

English arrows whistled across the moor to break the hushed stalemate. After a lengthy interval in which neither army was disposed to act, longbowmen from the English shires were ordered to advance and battle commenced.

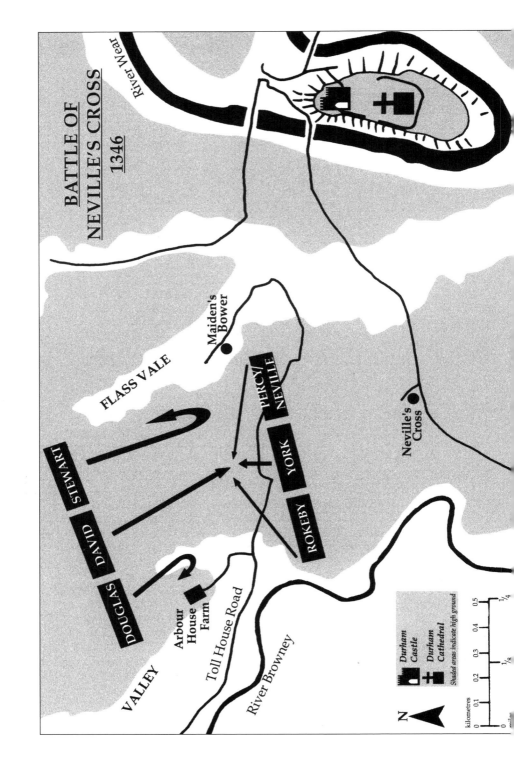

BATTLE OF
NEVILLE'S CROSS
1346

River Wear

FLASS VALE

Maiden's
Bower

STEWART

DAVID

DOUGLAS

PERCY/
NEVILLE

YORK

ROKEBY

Neville's
Cross

VALLEY

Arbour
House
Farm

Toll House Road

River Browney

N

kilometres
0   0.1   0.2   0.3   0.4   0.5

0   ¼
miles   ⅛

Durham
Castle

Durham
Cathedral

Shaded areas indicate high ground

Five hundred archers paced forward to fire but the Scots were ready. Given ample time to marshal their defensive formations, they closed ranks and the more adequately protected men-at-arms formed an enveloping metal carapace against the arrow fall.

With heads bent and covered in iron, densely drawn against the English attack, with helmets polished and shields fastened precisely, they withstood the arrows. Geoffrey le Baker, fourteenth century

But this disciplined forbearance in the face of a sustained attack, whilst it may have successfully avoided significant losses and exhausted the supply of English arrows, only irritated more adventurous Scotsmen. At Bannockburn a sudden charge had famously swept aside English archers. After being refused cavalry support, however, John Graham, Earl of Monteith, rode out alone from the Scottish front lines. With chivalric valour commended warmly by the Scottish Chronicler Wyntoun, 'good Sir John' galloped towards the flexing longbows to enable the Scots to 'fight more securely'. As they scattered from the path of the lance-waving knight, English archers brought down his horse, but not before Graham's recklessness had shown what might have been achieved if his request for one hundred horsemen had been agreed to.

Yet his fortunate return to the Scottish ranks may also have shamed his compatriots into action. King David's caution was at an end. Having survived the baptism of arrow fire relatively unscathed, he committed his main forces to the attack. Trumpets sounded across the moor and with spears levelled the Scots strode out to close the gap between the two great armies.

Almost immediately the Scottish right wing encountered severe difficulties. This formation, composed of three cohorts several hundred spearmen strong, was led by the Earl of Moray and William Douglas, who was no doubt keen to compensate for his earlier swingeing defeat at English hands.

A fearful fight between ditches and hedges. Walter Bower, fifteenth century

Possibly attempting an outflanking march, Douglas blundered again, not this time directly into the enemy, but down into the small but deceptively deep ravine which lies at the edge of Crossgate Moor. In contrast to the relatively open ground of the higher moorland, in 1346 this area was traversed by 'sikes' or ditches, through which the schiltrons now floundered. With some understatement Wyntoun describes their shambling progress as being 'discomforted'. Ever since that day this seemingly insignificant valley has caused problems, but only to generations of Arbour House farmers, unable to cultivate a scrubby yet historic wasteland.

Like Halidon, an ideal target had presented itself to English archers positioned on an overhanging slope. But unlike Halidon, their fire could not be of any great duration. With a parting flurry of arrows, the bowmen of Thomas Rokeby, Sheriff of Yorkshire, nimbly withdrew, avoiding being crushed in the iron press of two oncoming Scottish divisions. For the moment the longbows had achieved enough, however. A significant part of the Scottish

As they marched to battle from Bearpark, the Scottish army of King David II became 'ensnared between ditches'.

force had ceased to exist as an effective fighting unit. The corpse of one of its commanders, the Earl of Moray, lay in the bracken and any able survivors stumbled onto the moor to join their advancing comrades. Now it was the turn of English men-at-arms to prove their worth.

> *There was hard fighting; as men says,*
> *Such was never seen before those days.* Andrew Wyntoun, fifteenth century

If the English owed their victory at Halidon to the longbow, then they were equally indebted to the axe and sword at Neville's Cross. After the remaining Scottish divisions pressed home their assault, the savagery of hand-to-hand fighting was predictably intense. According to the Anonimalle Chronicle, 'lances were shattered, swords broken, armour pierced, helms and bascinets knocked off and shields broken into pieces.' For a long period it was a close

Neville's Cross, a battlefield panorama: from Toll House Road (left), to Arbour House Farm (centre), and Crossgate Moor (right).

fought contest with each side grasping and then losing the initiative. Several accounts agree that this confused and bitter melee continued over several hours, with the losses to both sides which that must imply. Yet in the midst of the bloodshed, curious chivalric rituals were not forgotten. By mutual agreement, fighting was suspended for rest and regrouping. Staggering back like battered pugilists, the tiring combatants 'rested from the fight for a time, leaning on their spears and weapons.'

Battle was resumed with refreshed brutality, but then the Scots, 'wearied by exertion, so terrified by the blows of axe heads', began to give way. Unambiguous reference to this particular weapon by the English chronicler Geoffrey Le Baker may be significant. Much of the Scottish infantry was armed with the twelve-foot-long spear, almost impregnable when employed as part of solidly grouped formations, especially against cavalry. But the spear was also unwieldy, requiring a fair level of practice to master, and virtually useless against an agile individual opponent. Then the Scots infantryman could be fatally slowed, forced to shorten or discard his spear and draw one of the personal weapons he may have carried. Moreover, fatigued by the lengthy battle on Crossgate Moor, the schiltrons may have found it increasingly difficult to close their ranks, allowing their companies to be fatally isolated by groups of English footsoldiers.

English success in this appears to have been aided by a measure of mobility and co-operation between battlefield units that the Scots could not match. In one of the more sober accounts of the fighting, Thomas Sampson relates that while English infantry and archers retreated twice, the line was held by men-at-arms who 'stood firm and fought stubbornly until the archers and footsoldiers reassembled.' They returned to action with a combination of archery volleys and 'whirlwind' infantry attacks against their faltering Scottish enemy.

Control of the battle was slipping further beyond Scottish reach. As well as attempting to weather the continuing attrition by axe and arrow, they then had to contend with the defection of a sizeable part of their army. At this crucial point, Robert Stewart and the Earl of March decided to play no further part in the battle. Not fully committing their division may have enabled them to survey the unfolding battle. Anticipating disaster, they 'escaped then, Home to Scotland', as diplomatically described by their compatriot Wyntoun.

They had added reason to run: Stewart to preserve his claim to the Scottish throne and the turncoat Earl of March to preserve his head from an English executioner's axe. His desertion was a crippling blow to the Scots, welcomed with barely suppressed satisfaction by Henry Percy: 'The cowardice of that traitor, who never dared to resist us in the field, profits our army more than the felling of a thousand Scots.'

Waves of English troops now lapped around the remaining Scottish division. At its collapsing centre, enclosed by a 'round tower' of loyal knights, King David of Scotland, English arrowheads embedded in his face, fought on. Several accounts maintain that he battled defiantly to a standstill, his bodyguard falling around him under the weight of English swords and axes, until he surrendered to John de Coupland, a hitherto unknown squire from Northumberland. More disparagingly, local tradition paints a craven Scottish king, rushing headlong from the battlefield to be discovered skulking under the arch of nearby Aldin Grange Bridge. But Coupland can definitely be credited with the king's capture. In the final tussle with David, the Northumbrian lost two teeth but gained the rank of a banneret and a fortune for his pains. A grateful Edward III, to whom he personally delivered his distinguished captive, rewarded Coupland with the immense sum of £500 a year for life. Similarly there is little doubt that David was in midst of the action on Crossgate Moor. Although he was fortunate to survive the attention of surgeons sent by Edward to treat his injuries, it is known that one of his arrow wounds troubled him for years to come.

> *The banners were still standing*
> *Face to face still fighting*
> *With all their force; but*
> *nonetheless*
> *Yet were they wholly vanquished.*
> Andrew Wyntoun, fifteenth century

Their king in custody and the battle lost, the surviving remnant of the Scottish army desperately attempted to escape. Some of them made despairing last stands but few reached their homes. As they straggled away many had the misfortune to be picked off by an English contingent which had arrived late for the battle. Others, managing to reach the border, were pounced on by the garrison from Berwick which lay in wait for them and harried them as far as the gates of Dunbar Castle. But most of the Scottish fugitives did not even begin this tormented bid for freedom. In Durham's Redhills, a wooded area on the eastern lip of Crossgate Moor, its name redolent of that violent day, many Scotsmen not considered worthy of ransom were brutally killed.

A clump of the woodland has, remarkably, survived through the centuries and in its midst lies the romantically named Maiden's Bower, a prehistoric burial mound. According to enduring local tradition, although not mentioned in Fossor's contemporary report to his bishop, on that extraordinary day in 1346, Prior John Fossor and his attendants from Durham Cathedral gathered on the small hill to pray for victory. For a talisman they brought with them a linen communion cloth from the coffin of Cuthbert. One of the most valuable relics of their patron saint, it was afterwards stitched into a red velvet flag which fluttered above northern troops as they marched to battle.

Legend portrays a defeated Scottish king fleeing from Neville's Cross to hide under the nearby bridge at Aldin Grange.

Maiden's Bower in Durham's Flass Vale. Monks prayed here while battle raged about them.

To offer thanks for the victory at Neville's Cross, a simple wooden cross was set on top of the Bower and it became a place of contemplation for monks on their way to summer retreat at Bearpark. Yet although this crude wooden memorial vanished long ago, other traces of the overwhelming English success in October 1346 can still be glimpsed around the cathedral and city of Durham.

Lord Ralph Neville was determined to ensure that his role in the great battle would not be forgotten. Like their adversaries, the Scots proudly carried banners and trophies into battle. One of the most renowned of these, the famed 'Black Rood', a small but wonderfully crafted golden cross, had been taken to London as a spoil of war in 1296. After the Durham battle, the Rood may have been presented as thanksgiving for the victory and deposited close to the shrine of St Cuthbert. Not to be outdone, Lord Neville probably then gifted a much larger and more splendid Rood. To display it fittingly, it was framed with russet-stained wainscoting decorated with gilded stars. Regrettably, all of these magnificent relics have long since disappeared, but high on the wall of the cathedral's south aisle, barely noticeable amongst the Romanesque grandeur, are slots cut into the pillars that once supported Neville's public display of generosity.

Fortunately, the memorial forever associating the Neville family name with Durham's most famed battle has survived. Neville's Cross monument stands incongruously in the precincts of a social club, a few yards east of the modern crossroads. A 'Nevillecrosse' marker is recorded to have stood near this place before 1346 but since then has endured several changes of form and location. After the battle, the original wayside cross was ornately decorated and embellished with Neville family crests. The completed stone pillar stood over twenty feet high until it was severely damaged by sixteenth-century vandals. They were possibly exploiting the disgrace of the once mighty Nevilles after their involvement in the failed 'Rising of the North' rebellion. As seen today, much of the monument is a patchwork of rough nineteenth-century masonry, although the blackened central stump is probably an ancient milestone. Only the socket base, which is chamfered and carved with crumbling reliefs of the Evangelists, remains of a once impressive construction, which was as much a symbol of aristocratic prestige as a celebration of an outstanding military victory. The monument is now ringed by a wall of spear-pointed railings, which, although distracting, are also somewhat appropriate. They are strangely evocative of the Scottish schiltrons that their young king saw broken on Crossgate Moor.

A 'most notable, famous and goodly larg cross of stonework'. Neville Cross as it may have appeared in the late fourteenth century.

Neville's Cross monument: cut down from its medieval splendour by some 'lewd and wicked persons'.

Although defaced and disturbed over the centuries, the Neville's Cross memorial can still be an evocative reminder of Durham's fiercest medieval battle.

After the battle, King David II of Scotland was held in relatively luxurious captivity in the Tower of London. He had eleven years in which to reflect on his benighted reign and he returned to a country wasted by plague and invasion and too exhausted to make war. England was similarly hard pressed by disease and for a while the North fought the Black Death instead of the Scots. The utter humiliation of David and his army at Neville's Cross was hoped by Prior Fossor to usher in an era which would 'end the painful discord' in Anglo-Scottish relations, and for more than two decades his aspirations were largely realised in much of Northumberland and Durham at least. But low-level hostilities continued to disturb the immediate border area, and in the summer of 1388, attempting to restore its tarnished military reputation, a Scottish army returned to fight on another wild northern moor.

After Neville's Cross, ostensible peace between its protagonists was marked by periods of truce. But, aided by their French allies, the Scots snatched Berwick back briefly in 1355, which brought Edward III down upon them, torching the land between Tweed and Forth during the infamous reprisals of 'Burnt Candlemas'. Within fifteen years, though, the protective zone England had established across lowland Scotland had been insidiously nibbled away. Only a segment of land straddling the border remained, with Berwick as ever its lynchpin. This revival in Scottish fortunes was due less to a monarchy which had no appetite for all-out war after their humbling on Crossgate Moor, than to the great lords of southern Scotland, the Earls of March and Douglas, whose nationalism was entwined with their own territorial ambitions. Ironically, this mirrored the situation across the border, where the northern counties had their own noble guardians powerful enough to counter the Scottish threat.

> *This battle that I treat of now was one of the sorest and best foughten without cowardice or faint hearts.* Jean Froissart, fourteenth century

As Edward III became embroiled with what would become a century of Anglo-French warfare, defence of the North became increasingly delegated to its leading families, particularly the Percys. Throughout the fourteenth century their power as Earls of Northumberland and Wardens of the Eastern Marches had steadily expanded. Their massive fortresses at Alnwick and Warkworth were on the northern fringe of a dynastic web of influence which stretched as far as the English court itself. Their strategic necessity to dominate the territories of their northern border was, however, frustrated by the unwelcome rivalry of a prominent Scottish neighbour. Both Percy and the Earl of Douglas fiercely contested ownership of extensive land tracts around Jedburgh and its forest area. The consequent personal animosity this added to traditional national divisions gave an extra cutting edge to their lethal meeting in the summer of 1388.

Cross-border friction had grown in 1384 after the expiry of another lengthy truce. As often, the starting of point of war was Berwick, which was fleetingly held by Douglas until the Earl of Northumberland marched to its relief. Hostility escalated in the following year. The capture of Wark by a Franco-

Scottish assault was answered by an invading English army. Accompanying it was the young King Richard II at the beginning of his disturbed and murderously terminated reign. The unpopularity of his regime at home was only amplified by his failure to bring a reluctant enemy to battle in Scotland. Furthermore, Richard's promotion of his uncle John of Gaunt in an attempt to dilute the power of the Earls of Northumberland was a recipe for English discontent which was savoured by the watching Scots. Their raiding cut-and-thrust, painfully familiar to the people of the North, returned.

> *The barons and knights of Scotland, knowing of this, determined on an inroad to England, as the opportunity was favourable now the English were quarrelling amongst themselves, to make some return for some of the many insults they had suffered from them.*
> Jean Froissart, fourteenth century

During July of 1388, in a sharp precursor to major campaigning, James, Earl of Douglas ranged unchecked through Northumberland to the walls of Tynemouth Castle. Shortly afterwards, in an obvious gesture of defiance to his adversaries in Alnwick, Douglas chose Jed Forest, the land he claimed as his own by gift from the Scottish monarch, as the place to congregate his troops for a more extensive strike against the English.

A combined Scottish attack was envisaged which would split the North of England in two. The Earl of Fife, son of the Scottish king Robert Stewart, rode on the western flank and Douglas traversed the Cheviot Hills through the windswept Reidswire Pass to descend towards the Percy den. Of the two Scottish wings, Douglas led a smaller, diversionary force, but it was compact and many of its men-at-arms were noted to be solidly clad with high-quality French armour. But they appeared to have little use for it as they plundered at will in Durham before turning northwards for the homeward leg of their profitable expedition.

Much of the English defence was concentrated in the west, where the Bishop of Carlisle and other local magnates forced the Earl of Fife back to Scotland after he had burned land in the north of Cumberland. To counter the unexpected Scottish raid in the east, a muster was under way in north Yorkshire, but with the Percys still ensconced in their castle at Alnwick, Douglas broke his return journey to test the fortifications at Newcastle.

Attempts to storm its well-braced walls by bridging the moat with brushwood were repulsed by alert defenders; but it is doubtful that this secondary wing of Scottish invasion was sufficiently well equipped seriously to jeopardise such a major bastion. Groups of knights may have indulged themselves in skirmishes outside the castle walls instead. This aristocratic sparring, described in a Scottish Chronicle as 'grand jousts of war by covenant', was not uncommon in siege warfare. In what was to become one of the most fabled of these incidents, Douglas was said to have clashed with Sir Henry Percy, who had been despatched from the fastness of Alnwick to superintend the belated English relief. In the furious melee Percy was unhorsed and his personal standard snatched from his fallen lance by the

South-east of Otterburn: the way to war. A view from the modern road towards the medieval 'drove road' which ran from Belsay to Elsdon.

The baronial Otterburn Towers was built in 1830, supposedly on the site of a peel tower which stood firm against the Scots in 1388.

Scottish commander. Jubilantly, he dared Percy to retrieve his colours in battle and the scene was set for a more telling contest to come. There can be no confirmation of this stirring tale of knightly chivalry, but equally there is no doubt that the Scottish proximity to the Percy estates would have been enough of a challenge for him to seek battle in any circumstances.

Failing to dent the defences of Newcastle, the Scottish raiders struck out for home on the morning of 18 August. A few miles from the town, at Ponteland, they found a less resilient tower and captured its custodian, Aymer de Athol. From there they continued on their well-beaten track, climbing steadily to the Cheviots and the border beyond. A day's march brought them up high on a broad riverside haugh of the Rede and the Northumbrian hamlet of Otterburn. Its peel withstood the Scots before they moved on to make camp on higher ground slightly north-west of the settlement. In the wooded area around Greenchesters, trees were felled to build a substantial rampart, signs of which it is claimed were still visible in the nineteenth century. In battle, however, this defensive precaution of Douglas was only short-lived.

The feast of St Oswald, 19 August, was drawing to a close as an English army, containing many retainers from the Percy household, hastened towards Otterburn. On a forced march from Newcastle, Ralph Percy had joined his older brother in the vanguard of the finally galvanised English response. They might initially have expected to catch a Scottish rearguard slowed by herds of stolen cattle. But now, warned by the local population, the English hot pursuit ground to a halt. The entire Scots army was encamped and at rest ahead of them.

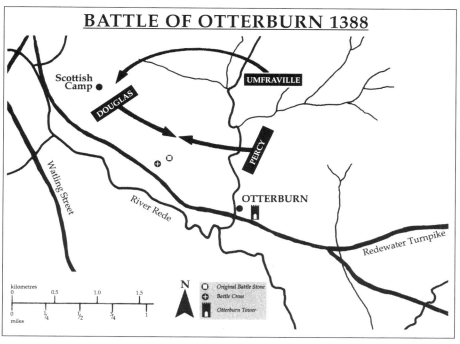

BATTLE OF OTTERBURN 1388

It was in August and fine and cloudless, and the air was calm and clear. Jean Froissart, fourteenth century

As shadows lengthened on that August evening in 1388, Lord Henry Percy pondered an uncomfortable choice. Pitched battle with its attendant confusion and unpredictability was in fact an exceptional occurrence in medieval warfare and often a final option for the commanders who fought it. To embark upon it in darkness was therefore unbelievably risky. Yet a Scottish army led by Percy's arch-enemy, who was apparently unaware of the English presence, lay close by. Clumps of birch and mountain ash which surrounded the Scottish barricades may also have shrouded the English advance. With all the impetuosity implied by his famed nickname, Harry Hotspur urged his men on to the attack.

A fierce battle began, with prodigious lance thrusts and men on both sides hurtling to the ground in this first clash. Jean Froissart, fourteenth century

Lacking targets in the failing light, the English archers stood aside to allow spear, sword and axe to carry the fight, as Percy's dismounted army swept into the periphery of the Scottish base and did not meet Douglas head on. Chronicle accounts suggest that many of the Scots had laboured through a day of summer heat to complete the earthworks of their camp and were now unarmoured but with their weapons to hand. Alerted by the growing din of combat in the lower camp they rushed to meet the attack.

Tradition holds that Harry Hotspur stormed across these fields in moonlight to surprise the Scots at Otterburn.

A bungled attempt to outflank the Scots only compounded Percy's misplaced opening gambit. Before battle commenced, an English detachment, claimed to have been led by Thomas de Umfraville, lord and protector of Redesdale, was flung out to the north. In what was intended to be a sweeping manoeuvre, which would encircle the unsuspecting Scots and drive against their rearguard, Umfraville instead lost precious time on a fruitless journey in the gathering darkness. Of Hotspur, Umfraville 'knewe nothyng whetherwarde he was gayn' and he failed to make contact with the main enemy force while his commander-in-chief was left to stem the flow of approaching Scottish footsoldiers.

With Percy struggling to hold the line, his right wing attracted an increasingly fierce Scots counterattack with Douglas in its front ranks. They swarmed around the exposed English flank, threatening it to force it back towards Otterburn. But then welcome relief arrived in the dark shapes of English men-at-arms. Umfraville's wandering column had groped their way back to the camp to buttress the crumbling English line.

Both armies grappled more closely together as the rage of battle intensified, illuminated periodically by the ethereal gleam of moonlight. In the confused havoc, combatants must have struck out against friend and foe alike. Indeed, intervals of total darkness compelled the fighting to be halted entirely.

When battle resumed, Douglas's huge battle standard, resplendent with his emblems of heart and star, became a rallying point for the Scots and an attractive prize for the strengthening English, who tenaciously pushed towards it. With a reckless abandon which could have been just as easily attributed to his opponent Hotspur, the Scottish commander was then reputed to have personally turned 'the tide of battle'. His standard-bearer son and three personal attendants struggling to keep pace, Douglas charged into the thickest part of the English ranks. Because he was not

> *Here also came the earl of Douglass, and with a great mace in his hand laied such fierce stokes round about him, that none came within his reach, but downe he went.*
> Ralph Holinshed, sixteenth century

fully armoured, however, possibly without bascinet or breastplate, his Homeric bravery was predictably short-lived. Swinging a great double-handed axe or mace, he scythed a path through the startled Englishmen until he was overwhelmed. Douglas would have been an invaluable captive, but without armour his noble status was probably unrecognised by the footsoldiers who struck him down.

His life had been sacrificed but his wild charge was a success. Rejuvenated by Douglas's desperate example, his hesitant comrades relaunched their offensive. Urging forward their division, Scottish knights Sir Patrick Hepburn and his son surged once more towards the central knot of fighting men. With lowered spears and piercing war cries, the regrouped schiltrons of the fallen Scottish leader rallied and also returned to the fray. A tide was now in flood powerful enough to wash the English away.

Mortally wounded by axe and spear blades, Douglas suffered one final indignity, trampled over as he was by the retreating English. Only his chaplain, Richard Lundie, lunging protectively with a spear, spared the Scottish commander further punishment. With his last words Douglas is said to have requested his loyal companion to conceal his death which would 'dishearten our own party or afford great encouragement to the English.' Yet even as his body was concealed by a cloak, the English were dealt the greatest discouragement of all.

By the fleeting brilliance of a harvest moon, heavy fighting continued. But any clear distinctions between opposing battle lines had by then dissolved into independent groups of thrashing combatants. In the midst of these Harry Hotspur was engaged in his own deathly struggle. His brother had earlier been captured and taken wounded from the battlefield. Now the younger Percy lost contact with his immediate supporters in the vicious melee. In single combat with Scottish knight Sir John Montgomery, Hotspur fought to a standstill before also surrendering his sword. Deprived of both charismatic leaders, defeat for the exhausted English was then almost inevitable. With the first pale streak of dawn the scale of their loss was revealed as the English survivors ran from the field. The ensuing rout was said to have stretched for five miles beyond Otterburn with the Scots seemingly more concerned with ransom than bloody retribution. Herding their prisoners before them, the victorious Scottish troops returned to their camp to mourn their leader and face one more English challenge.

> ... *without cowards or faynte hearts. For there was no other knight or sqyer but that dyde his devoyre [did his duty] and fought hande to hande.* Jean Froissart, fourteenth century

As Hotspur was escorted from Otterburn to await ransom at Dunbar, he could not know that the additional forces which might have swung the battle in his favour were advancing from Newcastle. In any case, the performance of these potential reinforcements, probably under the leadership of John Fordham, Bishop of Durham, was less than distinguished and was later to draw stinging censure from the authorities in London.

On the morning following the battle, Fordham's men did not even reach Otterburn. Their courage failed them when confronted by bleeding English survivors streaming from the battlefield. A return to Newcastle strengthened Fordham's complement but not its resolve to fight the Scots. On their second and final attempt, they are said to have approached the Scottish camp more closely, but seeing large numbers of English corpses piled around its still formidable ramparts and alarmed by the unearthly cacophony of Scottish signal horns, they completely abandoned their half-hearted attack.

Otterburn was left to its victors who buried their dead and prepared a special bier to carry Douglas to Melrose Abbey, where he was ceremonially entombed in the presence of his army. As they burned their camp and departed the site of their victory they marked it with the customary stone. 'Tumuli or sepulchres of the slain' are noted by Wallis in a history of Northumberland to have been still 'conspicuous' in 1769 but have since disappeared under the plough. The original battle stone, which may also have commemorated the spot where Douglas was killed, seems to have been uprooted to avoid a boundary dispute between a local landowner and the Duke of Northumberland, descendant of Harry Hotspur. In 1777, during construction of the Redewater turnpike, forerunner of the modern road through Otterburn, a new monument was erected in its present roadside position. Perhaps from then, in deference to the duke, the imaginatively rebuilt marker came to be misleadingly associated with the Percy name. A 'Douglas' Cross planted firmly in the Percy domain may have been an uncomfortable reminder of the frequency with which their family fought and died on the losing side.

Percy Cross at Otterburn: an ungainly collection of stones. Its socket may be from the original battlefield marker, but the tapering shaft above it, complete with iron hooks, was salvaged from a fireplace lintel at Otterburn Hall.

Otterburn's original battle stone, about three feet long, was removed in 1777 by Henry Ellison of Otterburn Hall before he constructed the present monument.

An unusual bench memorial, dedicated to the Battle of Otterburn. In 1888 it was placed beside the road, north-west of the battlefield, by W James, MP for Gateshead.

Elsdon St Cuthbert's. Rows of skeletons unearthed from its consecrated ground during the nineteenth century are likely to have been victims of the fighting at Otterburn.

Yet had he retained the initial element of surprise, Henry Percy could have scored a spectacular victory at Otterburn. But he had rushed an under-strength force from Newcastle and committed them to immediate action when food and rest might first have been more appropriate. In a lengthy contest against a possibly more numerous and fresher opponent, the exhaustion of Percy's troops had its inevitable consequence.

After a series of military disasters, a Scottish army had been triumphant at Otterburn in an epic nocturnal battle laced with enthralling tales of legendary valour, which ever since has been a rich source of inspiration for poets, painters and indeed historians alike. Above all, however, the defeat at Otterburn was the first major battle since Bannockburn in which it is clear that the English longbow played no significant role. When next called upon, however, English bowmen were not found wanting. Exploiting their deadly skills, Harry Hotspur took full revenge against his Scottish rivals in the Douglas clan. Once again Scotsmen would wilt as an English arrow storm broke above them.

Fragments displayed in the porch of the Church of St John the Evangelist at Otterburn are claimed to be remnants of the original battlefield stone, erected to mark the death in combat of James Douglas, Guardian of Scotland.

The Scots did not capitalise on their success at Otterburn. Brief Scottish raids against Carlisle and Berwick were successfully repelled before an Anglo-French truce of June 1389, which Scotland also adhered to, ushered in a period of relative but short-lived northern stability. Despite this, the local populations of the border regions, who always favoured loyalty to their kin before their country, continued to live by their own distinctively warlike code. Nevertheless, during the rule of Richard II, English policy towards a seemingly interminable conflict with their Scottish neighbours became outwardly pacific, attempting to sever the link between Scotland and France and conclude a separate *détente*. But the terms demanded by Richard were bitter to the Scottish taste. Feudal homage to an English monarch was still expected of the Scots and the ultimately hollow negotiations did little to defuse the potential for all-out war. Yet when conflict did break out again across the North, it was as much between great lords as great nations.

After the violent overthrow of Richard II in 1399, Scotland faced Henry IV, an English king who was more eager to fight than talk. His invitation to war came from the unlikely Scottish hand of George Dunbar, the Earl of March. After he had been snubbed by the Scottish monarchy and he had squabbled with the third Earl of Douglas, he defected to the English court and appealed for help from its king. Requiring no prompting, Henry immediately

The Unquiet Tyme of Kyng Henry the Fourthe. Edward Hall, sixteenth century

despatched the powerful Scottish magnate back to invade Scotland with the Percys for company in the early summer of 1400. These strange bedfellows initially achieved little but they thoroughly disturbed the Scottish hornets' nest and in 1402 the new Douglas, aptly dubbed Tineman ('the loser'), fell upon Northumberland in retaliation.

With English attention focused on rebellion in Wales, Douglas and several other major Scottish Lords led a powerful raiding force through Northumberland. Without any significant challenge, they stopped short at Newcastle before turning back for home heavily laden with their easily gained plunder. Following the path which claimed the life of his predecessor at Otterburn, Douglas then retreated towards hoped for escape through the distant Cheviots. But on this occasion the hills provided no welcoming haven for the Scots but became a charnel house for their scattered bones.

> *The same time the Scottes cruelly entered into England for they supposed all the lords beyond Humber to be occupied in all the parts of Wales.* John Stowe, sixteenth century

In contrast to the frenetic Otterburn campaign, the North appeared to be somewhat better prepared for invasion in 1402. Since open hostilities had been signalled two years earlier by the English with a futile expedition from Newcastle to Edinburgh, the Northumbrian authorities were on the alert against tit-for-tat raids into Northumberland, and a serious Scottish attack had already been dealt with proficiently by Sir Robert Umfraville. Thus the northern magnates maintained their vigilance, and on 14 September 1402 an army led jointly by the Percys and the Earl of March swung across north Northumberland to block the exit of the Scots.

Henry Percy in particular dared not repeat the botched night ambush at Otterburn which cost him eight months of freedom and gave conclusive victory to the Scots. Perhaps this concern, combined with the insight and experience of the Earl of March, at first helped to temper the usual Hotspur haste, as both men led their combined force to the outskirts of Wooler where the Scots had begun to bivouac. To reach their homes, the Douglas contingents would now have to march over the bodies of a defeated English foe.

Having first choice of battleground placed any medieval commander at a distinct advantage. At first displaying shrewd generalship, Lord Archibald Douglas gathered his schiltrons on the 1,000-foot-high slopes of Homilden, the 'bold bare hill' on Wooler's western approaches. But as he surveyed his enemy in the plain below him and battle drew on, his tactical judgement became increasingly unsound.

> *They [the Scots] chose a mountain near the toon of Wooler, called Halydowne Hill.* John Stowe, sixteenth century

Not overawed by Scottish monopoly of the higher ground, however, Percy and March simply crossed the valley to occupy the slopes of Harehope, about one mile to the north-west and opposite their watching enemy.

Given Hotspur's reputation for impatience, a Chronicle suggestion that he then immediately prepared to gallop uphill into the massed Scottish ranks has

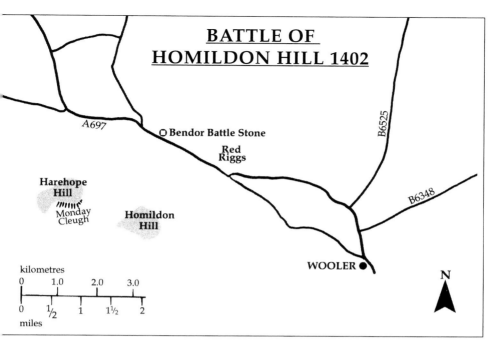

a ring of truth to it. Only the advice and restraining hand of his Scottish ally the Earl of March is alleged to have prevented a final charge to glory by the intemperate Northumbrian knight.

But with their composure restored the northern commanders instead compromised on a more dependable overture to battle. Intending to goad the Scots into a hasty attack, English archers trotted down the slopes possibly towards a large dry ravine, known as 'Monday Cleugh', and from there, aiming uphill towards the massed Scots, began to whip their shafts away.

> Without delay, our archers, placed in the valley, let their arrows against the Scots battle that they might by some means force them to come down. John Stowe, sixteenth century

It should not be overlooked that archers were also well represented in Scottish armies during this period and an English chronicler points out that they were deployed by Douglas as the engagement began. Historical debate has focused on the length of weapon they were armed with, but it seems clear that on Homildon, whatever variant of bow the Scotsmen drew, they were unable to reproduce the successful arrow barrage of their English counterparts, most of whom were Welsh recruits.

> On the other side, the Scottish archers let fly at our men, who yet, after they [the Scots] felt the grievous weight, as it had been a shower or tempest of arrows shot by the English men, they fled. John Stowe, sixteenth century

Remarkably, what had originated as an opening ploy by the northern forces was then allowed by the Scots to evolve into a sustained and severely damaging archery attack. Since their first assembly on the hillside, the Scottish army had been packed into a condensed block of men and horses, which perplexingly failed to disperse as the arrows began to fall and casualties began to mount.

Every volley of hardened steel-tipped barbs could not fail to find a mark in the claustrophobic Scottish ranks, which were said to be packed so densely that 'a breath of air could scarcely penetrate their files.' With no sign of retaliation against them the English longbowmen kept up their fire which fell as 'thick as hail upon the Scots'.

In his Chronicle, Walsingham writes effusively about the armour-piercing ability of the English clothyard arrows loosed on Homildon, claiming they passed cleanly through Scottish helmets. Modern research on the strength of armour from this period and the particular angle of arrow strikes required to penetrate it, however, has shown much of this to be anecdotal, making it likely that the 'perforated swords' and 'broken lances' that he refers to were probably caused by swingeing blows from pole-axes in close combat.

Despite this, the relatively well-armoured men-at-arms and their lightly covered horses, held ready for an anticipated charge, inevitably began to be injured by the uninterrupted fall of arrows which ricocheted around their crowded ranks on Homildon Hill. Poorly equipped spearmen, who formed a significant proportion of the Scottish force, fared much worse. With no instructions to do otherwise they stood and died at bay and the appearance of their afflicted formation was luridly described in a contemporary source as 'a huge hedgehog, bristling over with a thousand shafts, whose feathers were red with blood'.

Various theories have been offered to explain the passive stance of the Scottish leader during this wasteful carnage. One even suggests that, shocked by the ferocity and unexpected angle of the English arrow storm, Douglas became temporarily deranged. But as nothing can really be known about the motivation of the Scottish command structure during the battle, it is perhaps more helpful to suggest, prosaically, that Douglas was loath to be prised from his Homildon redoubt. The belief that the arrow deluge would quickly dry up led him to hold his ground as he waited for an inevitable English attack. Toiling up the defile towards him, Percy and his turncoat allies would then be promptly engulfed by the Douglas cavalry and rolled back down to be crushed in the valley below. But the English reserves of arrows were not yet exhausted and the longbowmen, emboldened by the immobile target which still lay at their mercy, advanced from the Cleugh to shoot again, decreasing their range and increasing their killing power.

Horses, maddened by the whistle of the continued archery fusillade and the cries of the wounded, kicked and bolted amongst the splintering Scottish ranks. Panic and dismay began to spread and with still no order for a cavalry charge, enraged Scottish knights were on the brink of mutiny.

Sir John Swinton, urging his countrymen 'not to stand like deer to be shot', is reputed to have been the inspiration for the long-delayed Scottish counterattack. In their darkest hour, old grudges amongst the Scottish knights were laid aside as they thundered down the slope. They were to be united in death. Freed from the arrow-bound duress on the bare hillside, Swinton careered towards the enemy with a company of about a hundred horsemen. The impetus of their charge punched through the first English ranks they met, but Swinton and many of his comrades were slowed to a halt and then cut from their saddles by the superior numbers of Percy's men who began to cluster around them. Spurring their horses, the survivors wheeled desperately back towards the Scottish lines. At last but too late, Douglas then went on the offensive.

Stung from his inertia, the Scottish commander waved his main force forward. The thrust of their attack was parried not by the English, however, but by a collision with the torn remnant of the earlier charge. Arrow fire too continued to torment them. Many of the English archers were still in place, protected from the horsemen by the rock-strewn gully and prehistoric ramparts which crease the lower slopes of Humbleton. Only when the Scottish infantry closed down on them

> *The encounter was sharpe, the fight was dangerous, the long continuaunce was doubtful.* Edward Hall, sixteenth century

did they retreat. Yet they fell back in good order. With undisguised admiration the chroniclers describe their disciplined movement, maintaining a steady

Bendor battle stone in 'Red Riggs' near Wooler. These gentle acres became killing fields for the Scots after they were routed at Homildon Hill in September 1402.

fire, as they filtered back through the ranks of their advancing English comrades. The work of the longbowmen was done and full battle began.

It was bloody but brief. Of the two armies that lashed at each other in the valley below Humbleton, Scotland's was the most disadvantaged. Weakened by a persistent archery assault and demoralised by the destruction of their initial cavalry attack, they broke and ran, pursued and struck down by Percy's horsemen, many of whom up till then had been little more than spectators. Much of the slaughter took place in Red Riggs, sloping farmland straddling the road at Low Humbleton from where numerous bones of men and horses have been uncovered. A trail of Scottish dead extended for thirteen miles to the River Tweed where a further five hundred were reputed to have drowned rather than face the vengeful English.

Over the centuries since the battle, the hill on which it was fought has become known as Humbleton and the fighting is commemorated by a hefty whinstone block, probably prehistoric, which stands isolated in a field near the tiny roadside hamlet of Bendor. Around here many of the Scots nobility who had been held back from the charge by their leader and fretted on the arrow-swept slopes, were eventually killed.

Though the tactical judgement of Lord Archibald Douglas may have been questionable, his valour was beyond reproach. Taken prisoner, he left the field at Homildon half-blinded and bearing five other wounds. But his caution at the outset of battle had played into the practised hands of Percy's archers:

> *In this battle no lord, nor knight, no squire gave any stroke to the enemies, but onely God gave the victorie to the English archers.* John Stowe, sixteenth century

It taxes credulity to accept the chronicler's overblown claim. The English success was plainly not due to archery alone. The Battle of Homildon may have been overshadowed by greater victories on more famous fields but from the mist-veiled hills of Northumberland in September 1402, one thing does remain clear. Another Scottish commander had been shown the folly of delay as his army was hamstrung by the rapidly firing English longbow.

Chapter 7

HOUSES AT WAR
1402–1496

... a smoke that rose in England, which after grewe to a great fire, and a terrible flame to the destruction of many a noble man. Edward Hall, sixteenth century

Extraordinarily, within a year of the Battle of Homildon, its embittered protagonists became brothers-in-arms. Hotspur and the Earl of Douglas made an opportunistic alliance before fighting together in an unsuccessful attempt to depose the English king. Like these two former northern enemies, their countries had reached an accommodation of sorts after the bloodshed in 1402. But it was an abeyance squeezed from the reluctant Scots. With so many of their nobility held prisoner in England, they would have been foolish to risk a resumption of major national conflict. Furthermore, a less febrile climate between the warring neighbours was encouraged by the appointment of Robert, Duke of Albany as Regent of Scotland. This hardened political veteran seemed intent to hold his fractious country together and he sent his soldiers to serve the French rather than fight on English soil. But he dared not curb the power of his southern lords and their continued designs on the border strongholds kept the North in the shadow of war.

Though tension had dampened down, the Scots demolished Jedburgh Castle in 1409 and began to venture further south. Sporadic raids ensued and while most went unrecorded, one has made a more substantial mark.

Yeavering lies tucked into the northern flank of the Cheviot Hills. Now sparsely occupied, this humble scattering of houses conceals a nobler past. Occupied since earliest times, Yeavering was once the site of an extensive hill fort settlement and a palace of ancient Northumbria. Later it was part of the estate of John de Coupland who won fame and fortune on the battlefield of Neville's Cross. During intervals of border warfare, however, Yeavering, exposed on the northern frontier, was often an early victim of the Scots.

On 22 July 1415, a substantial Scottish raiding party was intercepted here. Details of the resultant clash are fragmentary, but the intruders numbered enough to warrant an urgent English response. After the deaths in battle of the mercurial Hotspur and his father, the rebellious Percy family had not yet been restored to power and the protection of the North fell to Robert Umfraville and, ironically, the political enemy of the Percy house, Lord Neville, Earl of Westmorland and Warden of the West March.

Although outnumbered by a Scots force estimated at 4,000 men, Neville acquitted himself well. The English ranks, though apparently thin, contained a high proportion of bowmen and the Scots it is claimed were soon put to flight, sustaining heavy casualties and with many taken prisoner. As they had done at Homildon a dozen years before, the defeated Scottish survivors beat a headlong retreat over twelve tormented miles until they glimpsed the Tweed and the hope of deliverance.

Standing alone in a field at the foot of Yeavering Bell Hill is a six-foot-high column, traditionally held to mark the battle site. In common with similar markers it in fact predates by several millennia the fighting which later chanced to rage around it. Towards the end of the nineteenth century the whinstone monolith toppled over and lay neglected for decades. But it was raised again to recall a robust if unsung defence of Northumberland at the battle of 'Geteryne'.

Yeavering battle stone: distinctive monument for a forgotten battle.

For a quarter of a century after the repulse of the Scots at Yeavering, there was sporadic cross-border violence but no major campaigns. The flames that licked around Alnwick and Warkworth in 1449 were ignited as much by the resumption of Percy and Douglas feuding as the expiry of an Anglo-Scottish truce. Not until 1464 did English armies again advance through Northumberland. Then they marched north not to dislodge the Scots but to grab at the English crown.

England was riven with discontent during the reign of the Lancastrian King Henry VI. Popular revolt had almost brought him down in 1450 and aristocratic conspiracy fomented by the York faction battled to replace him as he lost his grip on his country and his sanity. By 1461 the red rose of York and the white of Lancaster had fought themselves to an exhausted standstill across Yorkshire and the South. Three years later their war spilled into the North.

The trobleous season of King Henry the Sixt. Edward Hall, sixteenth century

In swirling snow at the dreadful Battle of Towton in March 1461, the Lancastrian cause was dealt a crippling blow. From the slaughter, Edward, the Yorkist Earl of March, emerged with the English crown. But Lancastrian hopes were far from extinguished and Margaret of Anjou, wife of the ignored and imprisoned King Henry, became an able architect of their conspiracies.

> *[She] entered Northumberland, and toke the castle of Bamborough and stuffed it with Scottes.* Edward Hall, sixteenth century

Margaret retreated northwards, hoping to garner Scottish support and use northern fortifications to launch a Lancastrian revival. She was foiled at Durham Castle but more successful when she moved on into the pro-Lancastrian orbit of the Percys. Alnwick, Bamburgh, Dunstanburgh and Norham came under Lancastrian control and Berwick was handed to the Scots in exchange for their assistance. But the response of the Yorkist King Edward was irresistible. He was now in effective control of the English treasury and Margaret dared not face the massive army and impressive siege machinery which he could now field against her.

The queen's hopes were then further dashed against the forbidding rocks around Lindisfarne Island off the north-east coast. Along with her captain of mercenaries Pierre de Breze and a small French contingent, her ship was caught in a squall as she attempted to flee to Scotland. Margaret and de Breze made landfall at Berwick but many bedraggled French soldiers who survived the shipwreck were cut to pieces by a local militia. Margaret of Anjou's newly acquired Northumberland forts could expect further French support to be minimal as the Yorkist noose tightened.

Treachery amongst the nobility underscored the struggle for ascendancy in the north-east as much as it did elsewhere in this pernicious civil war. Both Ralph Grey and Ralph Percy shamelessly switched castles and allegiances between the rival parties. And in the early part of 1464 they were joined in Northumberland by Henry, Duke of Somerset, one of the most prominent of all these political contortionists. Originally an adviser to Queen Margaret, he now returned to the Lancastrian fold after his duplicity towards the House of York. United in deceit, all three men now embarked on a path towards their own destruction as they sought to salvage the Lancastrian lifeline to the Scots.

At Norham Castle, the alliance between Scots and Lancastrians had been strained to breaking point. Their combined army toiled for almost three weeks without success until they were beaten back by a Yorkist force commanded by the redoubtable Earl of Warwick. Queen Margaret left for Flanders, returning to England in 1471 for a last and tragic attempt to hold the throne for

> *... this manly woman, this coragious queen.* Edward Hall, sixteenth century

her hapless Lancastrian husband. Her sojourn in Northumberland would not be repeated. Ultimately she had found little consolation there but she was not forgotten and her forlorn meanderings around the county have been enshrined in the lore and landscape of Northumberland. Various sites are connected to a dramatic escape by the Lancastrian queen. A small stream near

Hexham, 'the Queen's Letch', is reputed to be where her horse stumbled, and close by is a roughly hewn out cave where it is supposed she took shelter from the Yorkist hue and cry. An engaging if unlikely story perhaps, but one that may have sprung from the sympathy felt in parts of the northern region for this loyal and determined woman.

In her absence the relief of Norham and the return of Berwick to English control encouraged the Scots to make peace overtures towards a resurgent House of York. Such a pact would have delivered the *coup de grâce* to Lancastrian designs in Northumberland, and the Duke of Somerset scurried towards Newcastle to sabotage the deal. The Neville Lord Montague, Warden of the East March, was entrusted to escort a Scottish delegation through Northumberland and Durham for peace talks in York. Determined that negotiations would never be opened, Somerset's small force of 'four score bows and spears' laid an ambush near Newcastle 'in a small wood'. But their target eluded them and, reinforced with a 'great fellowship' at Newcastle, Montague pushed on towards his rendezvous with the Scottish envoys at Norham.

Boosted by men from the garrison at Alnwick, a Lancastrian force, led by Lords Percy, Hungerford and Ros hurriedly blocked the Yorkist path at Hedgeley Moor, on the Roman causeway about six miles south of Wooler. This area of open moor was a sensible choice for a Lancastrian stand, broad enough on which to deploy and affording a generally clear vista towards the south. But an early sight of their approaching opponents seems to have been enough for Hungerford and Ros. It appears that the marching Yorkist ranks were much more numerous than the diplomatic escort they had anticipated and the perfidious nobles withdrew their soldiers from the

In his journey he was countered by the Lord Hungerford, the Lord Roos, Sir Rauf Percy, and divers other at a place called Hegely Moor. Edward Hall, sixteenth century

Hedgeley Moor: beginning of the end for Lancastrian hopes in the North.

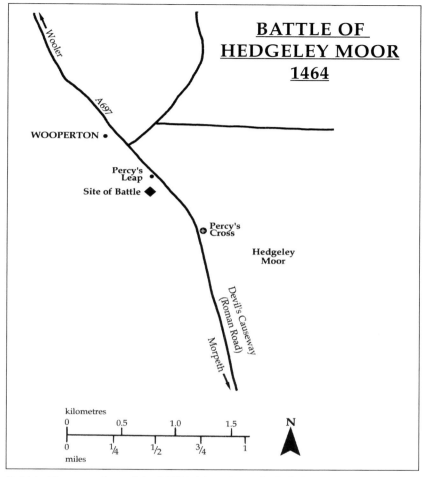

BATTLE OF HEDGELEY MOOR 1464

Wooler

A697

WOOPERTON •

Percy's Leap •

Site of Battle ◆

⊕ Percy's Cross

Hedgeley Moor

Devil's Causeway (Roman Road)

Morpeth →

kilometres
0   0.5   1.0   1.5
0   ¼   ½   ¾   1
miles

N

field 'without stroke striking'. With his retinue, Sir Ralph Percy stood alone to face the oncoming Yorkist force commanded by Sir John Neville, the Lord Montague.

During the previous decades it must have been galling for Percy to watch the Neville family's steady accumulation of power and prestige. It had culminated in the heady political influence exerted by Montague's brother Richard, Earl of Warwick, the so-called 'Kingmaker'. On 25 April 1464 at Hedgeley Moor, Ralph Percy's rivalry with this branch of the Neville dynasty was brought to a deadly conclusion.

Only bare details of the battle survive. It seems to have been brutal and brief. Hopelessly outnumbered, Percy apparently went some way towards resurrecting a reputation tainted by his earlier deceptions and fought to the

Boulders, thirty feet apart, are reputed to mark Ralph Percy's leap to glory at the battle of Hedgeley Moor.

Hedgeley Moor: emblazoned with family emblems but shorn of its head, another Percy Cross stands on a Northumbrian battlefield.

end. Accompanied only by his die-hard corps of personal retainers, Percy remained on horseback. Cutting at his surrounding foes, he led a desperate charge until his horse was struck by arrow fire. In its death throes the animal bounded ten yards through the air before throwing its wounded master, who was finished off on the ground. Two weather-beaten stones adjacent to the modern road still measure out the prodigious 'Percy's Leap', and a finely decorated square sandstone pillar is reputed to cover the site of Ralph Percy's gallant final moments. 'I have saved the bird in my bosom,' are said to have been his dying words: an obscure allusion to the Lancastrian king to whom Percy had recommitted his allegiance. It is a tale possibly intended to mitigate the previous disloyalty of this nonetheless intrepid warrior.

Percy's victorious opponents were certainly deemed to have been impressed with his courage as they trooped from the battlefield 'with full sorry hearts' to continue their violently interrupted expedition to Norham. Yet nothing is known of the participation of the senior Lancastrian leader in the fighting. Indeed, the Duke of Somerset may have earlier split his command and was perhaps not present at Hedgeley Moor. But it is certain that, barely two weeks after the destruction of the Percy contingent, he was given one more opportunity to prevent Yorkist supremacy in Northumberland.

Successfully completing his mission by delivering his Scottish charges to York, Lord Montague returned to his unfinished business in Northumberland. Although many northern castles remained in Lancastrian hands, Newcastle, captained by Lord Scrope, still flew the Yorkist colours and became a starting point for Montague's thrust towards the west. Here Somerset was marshalling his forces for a battle it was imperative he must not lose. Furthermore, without Margaret of Anjou, the flagging Lancastrian cause had to rely on her ailing husband as a figurehead of support. Henry VI was known to have stayed at Bywell on the Tyne during this time. With his enemy bearing down upon him, however, such was his urgency to abandon the riverside castle that he was said to have left behind his helmet. It was encircled with the English crown he was unfit to wear.

The massive gatehouse tower at Bywell Castle, part of Ralph Neville's ambitious but unfinished fortification guarding the River Tyne. Henry VI's helmet 'cum corona et gladio' (with his crown and sword) was discovered here before the Battle of Hexham in 1464.

Throughout the tribulations of their expedition, the Lancastrians appear to have received the most consistent backing in the western districts. Tynedale remained their most dependable region and, fittingly perhaps, its major town Hexham became a headquarters and last staging post for a Lancastrian revival in Northumberland. Anticipating that the Yorkist army would cross the Tyne downstream at Corbridge and stab at Hexham's exposed underbelly, Somerset therefore waited in the south-west approaches of the town. In this position he could guard the main fording points on the Devil's Water, a tributary which runs rapidly north-east towards the Tyne and throws a crooked but strong defensive arm around Hexham.

> *This battle called Exham field.* Edward Hall, sixteenth century

Amongst many engagements in over thirty years of fighting during the Wars of the Roses, the events at Hexham on 15 May 1464 are amongst the least documented. Consolation can be taken, though, that the general area over which the battle was fought has remained largely unspoilt. From this verdant Northumbrian landscape of steep valley and tumbling stream, the probable

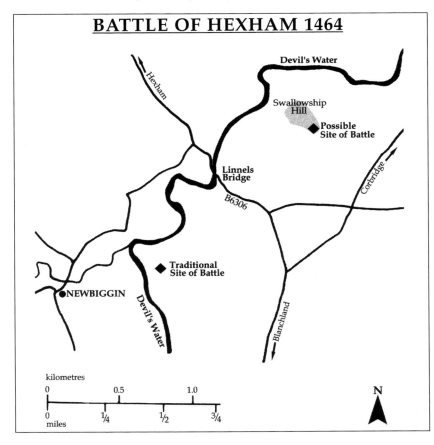

BATTLE OF HEXHAM 1464

Devil's Water

Hexham

Swallowship Hill

Possible Site of Battle

Linnels Bridge

B6306

Corbridge

Traditional Site of Battle

NEWBIGGIN

Devil's Water

Blanchland

kilometres
0   0.5   1.0

0   ¼   ½   ¾
miles

N

course of battle may still be gleaned.

Tradition says that the Battle of Hexham took place on the Levels, a meadowland area of riverside haugh less than three miles from the centre of Hexham. Enclosed to the north and west by a stretch of the Devil's Water, this flat, well-watered and protected enclave would provide a first-rate campsite for an army but it could also become a death trap in a major battle. A Victorian historian suggested that Somerset deliberately selected such an impractical battle site with no avenue of escape to discourage his command from desertion in the face of the enemy. It is hard to believe that the Lancastrian leader would have risked his precious army and his cause in this way. It is therefore easier to agree with more recent scholarship which suggests that he drew his men up on higher ground slightly towards the north-east of the present-day Linnels Bridge. From Swallowship Hill, one mile from the generally accepted battle location, Somerset would have strategic control of three major river crossings and have clear sight of his oncoming enemy.

> *… encamped in a faire plaine called Lynels in the water of Douill in Exhamshire.* Edward Hall, sixteenth century

There is no doubt about the result of the battle which followed, wherever it was eventually joined. One chronicler describes Hexham as 'a sore fought field' but all concur that, like Hedgeley Moor, it resulted in utter defeat for the Lancastrians, although on this occasion unrelieved by any memorable deeds of chivalric valour. If they escaped the Yorkist billhooks, Somerset's routed men must have

> *The lord Montacute, criying on his men to do vauliantly, entered by plain force, the battaill of his enemies, and brake their array.* Edward Hall, sixteenth century

The Levels: widely considered to be the location of the Battle of Hexham in 1464, they could also have become a lethal trap for the beaten Lancastrian army.

Control of higher ground on Swallowship Hill may not have helped Somerset to hold back the Yorkist army at Hexham. (Duke's House can be glimpsed on the horizon.)

Linnel's Bridge near Hexham Levels was rebuilt about 1698. It spans the Devil's Water, an awkward obstacle on any Lancastrian dash for freedom.

Hexham: Duke's House, built in 1873 on a site alway associated with the final journey of the defeated Lancastrian commander.

The precincts of Hexham's Priory Church, burial place of the executed Duke of Somerset in May 1464.

scattered back towards their base and plunged into the cold Devil's Water which hemmed it in.

Overall fatalities may have been relatively few, as no Chronicle record of high-born casualties exists. But the captured Yorkist nobility definitely fared badly in the aftermath of defeat. A wounded Somerset was reputedly conveyed to a local cottage, which, even after it was supplanted by a Victorian gothic mansion, has retained its local name as the 'Duke's House'. Yet if he was sheltered there it was a fleeting reprieve. King Edward's earlier leniency towards his double-dealing lords was at an end. Within hours the Duke of Somerset's head was displayed in Hexham market-place.

After their army had been smashed at Hexham, the last pockets of Lancastrian resistance in Northumberland were rapidly mopped up. Alnwick and Dunstanburgh capitulated without much of a fight and only Bamburgh required the destructive intervention of the Yorkist trio of hefty artillery pieces, 'London, Dijon and Newcastle'. From the debris of the castle walls an injured Sir Ralph Grey was taken to receive the punishment which Edward thought fitting for 'that fals traytor'.

> *... stones of the walles flewe unto the see.* Warkworth's Chronicle, fifteenth century

By the time of his execution most other prominent Lancastrian leaders of their northern rebellion, including Ros and Hungerford, who had abandoned Ralph Percy so dishonourably at Hedgeley Moor, had been similarly dealt with. From the outset their attempt to build a power base across the northern counties was doomed to failure. The Lancastrians were unable to translate their hold on the major castles of Northumberland, obtained as much by conspiracy as seigecraft, into distinct territorial gain. With greater resources of material and manpower seemingly always at his disposal, King Edward was able to isolate and ignore the northern fortresses and sweep aside any force the Lancastrians could summon against him. His victory in Northumberland

Alnwick Castle: a home of the Percy dynasty and heart of Northumbria's defence. During the Wars of the Roses it was merely a pawn in a deadly game of deception.

Bamburgh Castle: built for bygone wars. Pulverised by cannon in 1464, it became the first English castle to fall to artillery fire.

marked the beginning of a brief respite for the House of York in its long battle for the English throne.

Scottish interference was markedly absent during the later stages of this upheaval in the North. They were placated with the custody of Berwick but a more equable stance by their monarch James III also kept the border relatively quiet. Yet his enemies grew impatient with what they perceived to be a rule of benign neglect. His brother Alexander was installed by the English as Scottish regent and in return for their aid restored Berwick to 'the southron fold'. On 24 August 1482, after centuries of unabated wrangling with untold loss of life, this maltreated town changed hands for the thirteenth and final occasion. An English Berwick was not fought over again but the 'auld' argument still had longer to run.

More threatening border disturbance came with a new Scottish king. James IV continued to explore English weakness at times of internal political crisis, and in 1496, to back the pretender Perkin Warbeck, Scottish forces entered Northumberland. Until 1513, however, James needed little more than warlike posturing. Then he led Scotland's last great feudal levy in a desperate tilt at the waiting English ranks.

Chapter 8

FLOWER OF SCOTLAND
1503–1603

In the early years of the sixteenth century an Anglo-Scottish truce was signed in a treaty and sealed by a marriage contract. But while the union between James IV of Scotland and the English Mary Tudor did bear fruit, the alliance between their countries barely outlived its infancy. Initially, an element of official co-operation did exist and enhanced attempts were made by the authorities to control their respective border populations. However, even summary execution through liberal application of the draconian 'Jeddart Justice' failed to permanently suppress the lawlessness of many of its hawkish clans.

Yet border disruption did not cause the eventual break between the countries. James IV had gained the most from the relative suspension of military activity which had existed between them. It had helped make possible an enlightened reign of considerable cohesion and stability for Scotland. A pious man, the Stewart king also cultivated links to Europe and the papacy to enhance his country's prestige. But his royal English brother-in-law had much more grandiose continental ideas.

From the beginning of his reign in 1509, Henry VIII clearly stated his intention to wear the French crown as well. After France annexed northern Italy, European disorder escalated and Henry grabbed at the opportunity to fulfil his ambition. But by joining the 'Holy League', a papal coalition to bring the declared French heretics to heel, he also plunged the 'auld alliance' into crisis. As a matter of course, Louis XII of France reminded Scotland of their mutual obligations. Then, as the situation deteriorated, Louis increased the urgency of his pleas for assistance and the amount of

> *For the Scottes are the shaft and dart of the Frenchmen to shote and cast at their pleasure against the English nacion.*
> Edward Hall, sixteenth century

money he would pay to secure it. On several occasions the Scottish king, mindful of the delicate relationship with his powerful English neighbour, diplomatically fended off the French requests. A famed turquoise ring and romantic entreaty from the French queen was said to have finally swayed him to invade England on her country's behalf. But undoubtedly as attractive was her husband's pledge of 50,000 francs and extensive military support for the great venture. In early August of 1513, the Rubicon was crossed. Henry's personal mission to chastise the French was rudely interrupted by an ultimatum from James commanding the English king to 'desist from further invasion'. Unsurprisingly, the demand was angrily dismissed. The 'Perpetual Peace' of James's marriage contract had lasted eleven years.

For the Scots, the campaign could not have had a more inauspicious beginning. Riding south from the border with a force of possibly 7,000 men, Lord Alexander Home, Warden General of the Scottish marches, burnt seven

And when they were nere assembled, they brought themselves into a brome felde, called Myfeld, where the Scottes should pause. Edward Hall, sixteenth century

Northumberland villages. On 13 August 1513, his plodding retreat, hampered by a large herd of stolen horses, was halted on Milfield plain, six miles to the north-east of Wooler. Concealed in roadside trees, a contingent of English bowmen led by Sir William Bulmer of Brancepeth Castle lay in ambush. One shredding volley of arrows appears to have been enough for the surprised Scots. Hundreds were swept down by English archers who 'shotte so holy together.' Although Home escaped from the subsequent disintegration of his column, many were held captive and his battle standard was seized as an English prize. A Chronicle tale relates that James ignored a mysterious harbinger of disaster who appeared before him about this time. The Scottish king seems to have been similarly unmoved by a very real defeat inflicted on his forces by a numerically inferior English army at Milfield. Only later was the ominous significance of this 'Ill Raid' acknowledged.

Yet James's confidence was well founded in 1513. In common with other European monarchs of that period, he strove to keep pace with developing

The Scottes daily shipped long speres called colleyne clowstes armure and artilerie. Edward Hall, sixteenth century

military technology. The Scottish king's seventeen-gun artillery train was amongst the most modern available and since 1496 his new workshop in Stirling had been producing good-quality plate armour in significant quantity. Above all James could not fail to be impressed by the Swiss way of war which had swept all before it on the continent. Unbeatable in battle throughout the later fifteenth century, the Swiss or 'Almeyns' tactical approach was based upon highly trained and strictly disciplined infantry formations. These were equipped with an 18-foot-long pike and were supported by outrangers armed with an assortment of crossbows, halberds and small bore handguns. They were immovable under attack but could then advance at a deceptively quick pace, rolling over their enemy with overlapping phalanxes of three units in formations not dissimilar to the traditional Scottish schiltron. Scottish legislation signalled the adoption of the pike in 1471, but it was not until war with England was imminent that large stocks of the weapons began to be shipped from the Low Countries.

Experienced French captains arrived with them but the time to drill their Scottish hosts was short. Nevertheless, on 22 August 1513, James IV crossed into Northumberland and marched towards oblivion on Flodden Field with the most powerful Scottish army ever seen.

Reduction of the border fortresses in the Till valley was the Scots' first objective. Confident in the solidity of his castle and the stockpile of his supplies, John Anislow, the constable of Norham, rashly dared the Scottish king to do his worst. Scots Master Gunner Robert Borthwick then demonstrated that advances in the gun founder's craft were rendering all castles obsolete. According to an English Chronicle, after five days of thunderous cannonade and 'three great assaults', the Bishop of Durham's great bastion at Norham was 'compelled to yield.' Wark and the lesser forts at Ford and Etal cared not to share in the fate of the ruined and plundered Norham and hastily conceded defeat. In the cold wind and rain of an early autumn, James sought shelter and, according to his detractors, female companionship at Ford. With the castles secured and the season for campaigning almost at an end, he could afford to relax. The act of invasion had discharged James's duty to the French and despite considerable desertions his army remained strong enough to withstand any English response. On the ridge top of the neighbouring Flodden Edge, Scottish soldiers began to dig pits and haul their huge guns into position.

The English commander-in-chief might also have been affected by the inclement weather. It no doubt aggravated the rheumatism which was known occasionally to force him from horseback into a less than martial carriage ride. Entrusted with defence of the North in his seventieth year, however, the vastly experienced Earl of Surrey's vigour and enthusiasm for command seemed to

Ford Castle: headquarters of James IV on his last campaign and burnt before he left for Flodden.

Norham Castle: of such strategic value, this 'Queen of Border Fortresses' was restored by Thomas Ruthal, Bishop of Durham, after it was wrecked by the Scots in August 1513.

Norham Castle: pounded by Scottish artillery in 1513. Now under repair to withstand a new millennium.

be undiminished and from his headquarters at Pontefract he busied himself with preparations to combat the Scottish invasion. He had almost crossed swords with James IV at an earlier siege of Norham eighteen years before. Now in the twilight of his career, Thomas Howard, Earl of Surrey was determined to punish a Scots king whose invasion had prevented him from fighting at the side of Henry VIII in France.

Waiting on Surrey's orders for mobilisation were the four northern counties as well as the levies of Lancashire, Yorkshire and Cheshire held back from the army that had sailed for France. Although substantial, this reserve may still have fallen somewhat short of the massive Scottish force.

Unlike his Scottish counterpart, Henry VIII had not invested so heavily in the latest weaponry. He was interested in modern artillery, but his best guns were in France and his army was left to rely on tactics and equipment largely tried and tested in earlier decades of almost continuous fighting. The deployment of archers to pave the way for dismounted men-at-arms and spearmen continued to dominate the English battle plan. But the flexibility of its archery component, first glimpsed at Neville's Cross, was clearly confirmed at Agincourt in 1415 by bowmen who after withdrawing from the front line then darted back into close-quarter action, launching lethal attacks with knives, swords and skull-crushing lead hammers or 'mells'.

Similar adaptability was evident in other weaponry of Surrey's army, which now began to muster at Newcastle. Pikes of the Flemish pattern were not widely in use by the English footsoldier, but by the Wars of the Roses his traditional brown bill had undergone a particularly English evolution. Modified from a basic farming implement resembling a hedging tool, the English billhook had become a remarkably effective weapon. At eight feet in length it was dwarfed by the Scottish pike but its cutting and stabbing combination of curved and pointed blades excelled in the close combat of visceral 'hand strokes' in which it would soon be employed.

Before he arrived at the Tyne to take full command, Surrey had stopped at Durham to gather in the soldiers of the Palatinate and collect the revered Banner of St Cuthbert which for centuries had flown above them on their march to battle. By 4 September, in fields at Bolton to the west of Alnwick, the English army, bolstered by 1,000 men spared from the fleet, began to array into battlefield formation. A vanguard composed of three divisions was placed under the command of

> *The same daye my Lorde devyded his Armie in two bataylles that is to wytte in a vaunward and a rerewade.*
> Trewe Encountre, sixteenth century

Thomas Howard, Lord Admiral of England, while his father the Earl of Surrey led a similarly structured but smaller rearguard. The following day 20,000 men saw the Red Dragon of England raised above them as Surrey quickened the pulse of war.

Urgency had underscored all his preparations. Not only was he concerned that James would step back across the border to defy him as he had done in 1497, but Surrey also knew that dwindling supplies could end the English campaign before a shot was fired. Consequently, Surrey then despatched his herald Rouge Croix to offer battle and 'try the rightness of the matter by Friday at the farthest.' To ensure the Scottish king did accede to this polite request, an accompanying note from the Lord Admiral was couched in more insulting tones designed to goad the Scots to fight. The day was fixed but not the place. Inconveniently for the English, James refused to descend to Milfield plain and engage in a more gentlemanly contest. Protected to the west by a bog and to the east by the sluggish but deep River Till, the long ridge of Flodden Edge which James commanded was studded by his arsenal of cannon. It would take much more than appeals to an outdated code of chivalry to bring him down.

Surrey had moved his army close to the southern approaches of Wooler, within striking distance of the Scottish position. On the preceding day to that appointed for battle, he marched his army to the north and away from Flodden. His troop movements initially obscured by high ground around Barmoor, Surrey began to outflank his enemy. In a bold manoeuvre, ever since

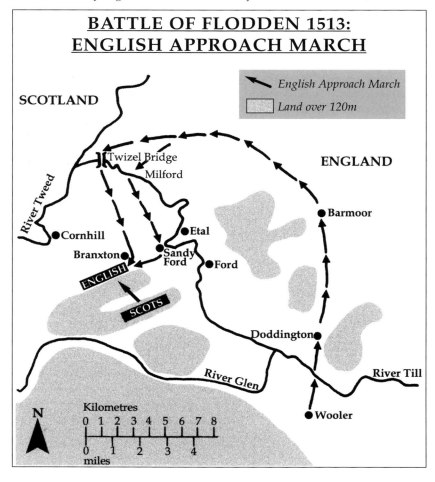

BATTLE OF FLODDEN 1513:
ENGLISH APPROACH MARCH

applauded by military strategists, the veteran English commander looped behind the south-facing Scottish redoubt, wedging his army between James and a homeland he would never see again.

At first light on Friday, 9 September, after an uncomfortable night rationing out their inadequate supplies in Barmoor woods, a hungry English army moved to battle. To complete the ambitious encirclement Surrey needed to get them swiftly and safely across the Till where they might be vulnerable to a snap Scottish attack. Dividing his force, Surrey sent the vanguard and its artillery train towards Twizel, where under the command of Lord Thomas Howard they squeezed across the single arch of Twizel Bridge high above the Till. For over an hour they clattered over the narrow parapet, reaching the southern riverbank without challenge. Rather unfairly perhaps, King James has been maligned for his inaction at this perilous stage of the English operation. Only when his army turned back towards the Scots, however, did Surrey's intentions finally become clear. Indeed, so perplexing was the English route that some members of James's council believed it was destined for Berwick where Surrey could reprovision prior to a counter-invasion of Scotland. But James appears to have remained sanguine throughout the speculation concerning English tactics. After all, on the heights of Flodden Edge the Scottish king literally still held the upper hand. It was only when it was suggested by his nobles he should not take part in the fighting that he became enraged. His resolve was unshaken to 'fight this day with England.' He would presently be granted his wish. Downstream from Twizel Bridge Surrey led the rearguard across the Till to link with the main body of the English army.

> *The Lord Hawarde at 11 of the cloke the said nine day, passed over the brigge of Twyselle.* Articules of the Bataille, sixteenth century

By mid-afternoon only one more serious natural obstruction taxed Surrey as his army thronged the fields and tracks around Branxton village and its hill to the rear of the Scottish position. Local guides must have directed the English to the 'Branx' causeway which bridged the Pallinsburn, a seemingly innocuous stream concealing a broad swathe of marshy terrain which would have mired the twenty-three English artillery pieces. Once safely across, they could await the rearguard which was skirting the soft ground as they advanced towards the English objective of Branxton Hill.

But then smoke from the burning rubbish of their abandoned camp began to clear and Scottish flags appeared. At last realising that a rearward attack by the English was under way, James had been grudgingly forced from Flodden Edge. By moving one mile north to Branxton Hill he denied its lofty slopes to Surrey's army who instead deployed across a lower ridge. Rotating a cumbersome army and hastily uprooting heavy cannon to ill-prepared positions was an impressive logistic achievement on the part of the Scots king. Yet this paled to insignificance when compared with Surrey's tactical coup. The level of organisation and discipline of the Englishmen who had made it possible augured well for the desperate struggle to come.

Confronted by the Scots, in 'four great battles', dense squares which

Flodden Field: a slippery descent for the Scots from the crest of Branxton Hill.

The ditch and stream at the foot of Branxton Hill: troublesome hurdle for the Scottish infantry in 1513.

menacingly lowered their pikes towards him, Thomas Howard at the forward tip of the vanguard, urged his father to close up the English line. So hasty was Surrey's response that Edward Stanley and part of his shire contingent received no order from their commander-in-chief. They became detached from the main force and did not arrive until fighting was well advanced. Fearing an immediate Scottish attack, Surrey could not delay, however, and to mirror the Scots rapidly formed a fourth battle. With the horsemen of Lord Dacre gathered behind them at Branxton Church, the reorganised English line stretched out for almost a mile towards the south-west. At its centre, in the vanguard of the Lord Admiral on Piper's Hill, were the soldiers of Northumberland and Durham. Flying above them was the red velvet banner of Cuthbert.

Between four and five o'clock in the afternoon, the Battle of Flodden began with a blare of trumpets and the roar of cannon. Thunderously confirming the changing face of warfare, rival artilleries duelled with each other across a static battlefield. Of the salvoes that were fired, however, few from the Scots side appear to have been on target. Their weighty cannon, more appropriate for blasting at castle walls, were slower to load and more difficult to range and may also have been hamstrung by a hasty and poorly sited relocation. The

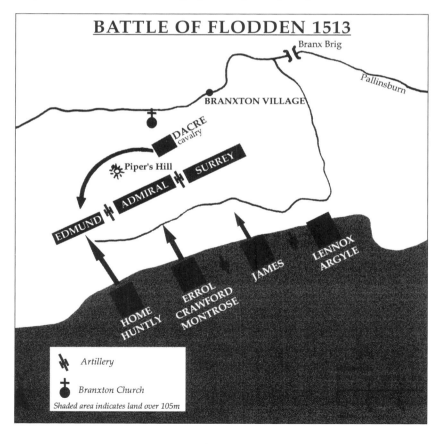

BATTLE OF FLODDEN 1513

Branx Brig

Pallinsburn

BRANXTON VILLAGE

DACRE cavalry

Piper's Hill

SURREY

ADMIRAL

EDMUND

HOME HUNTLY

ERROL CRAWFORD MONTROSE

JAMES

LENNOX ARGYLE

Artillery

Branxton Church

Shaded area indicates land over 105m

English batteries enjoyed more success as their carriages were more mobile and the lighter guns they carried more suited to field engagements. One of their fusillades is often reported to have scored a direct hit on a Scottish gun crew, killing Robert Borthwick, King James's esteemed Master Gunner. Borthwick in fact survived the battle but there is no reason to doubt the relative accuracy of the English artillery which fired towards him and his gun teams. Hurtling uphill, round shot from the English 'falcon' guns skipped along the soft surface tearing gaps in Scottish ranks more used to a rain of arrow shafts falling from above.

> *Then oute braste the ordinaunce on both sides with fyre flamme and hydeous noyse.* Edward Hall, sixteenth century

Unwilling to sustain further losses and probably disappointed with the blunt cutting edge of his cannon technology, James resorted to more conventional ways of battle. His vanguard of 10,000 'borderers and countrymen' led by Lord Home and the Earl of Huntly moved steadily on to the attack. This was not the frenzied onslaught of impetuous Highlanders featured in some traditional accounts, however, but a controlled and steady assault. The pike echelons had done well to remember the lesson in continental tactics from their French advisers and according to a commentary possibly written later by the Lord Admiral himself 'came down the hill and met with them in good order in the Almayns manner.' Within a short time, all of the Scottish army, their four great battles in staggered formation, a bowshot between each, descended towards the English lines 500 yards away.

On the left, leading the way were Lord Home and his border pikemen supported by Lord Huntly and the Gordon clansmen armed with a fearsome array of claymores, axes and bows. As the Scots closed the gap, the English falcons, effective within 1,800 paces, were firing at close range and the two-inch diameter metal balls they spat out would kill and maim. But at 200 yards, the Scots came under a more familiar bombardment.

In the Tudor era, archery continued to be a valued part of the English war machine. Stacks of bow staves recently dredged up in the Solent from the wreck of Henry VIII's flagship, the *Mary Rose*, clearly confirm this. Yet Flodden's early arrow shower seems to have been easily weathered by the leading Scottish ranks. James's armourers had done their work well and thanks to their allies the Scots may also have been equipped with 'pavishes', broad wooden canopies under which they could shelter. English chroniclers blamed their bowmen's rare failure on inclement weather which undoubtedly had a detrimental effect upon the longbow's performance. Yet English archers would do everything they could to counter this, probably not stringing their bows until the last possible moment. It should also be remembered that Cheshire and Lancashire troops, many of them bowmen, were still scurrying towards the battlefield's eastern flank where they would soon make their presence felt on the Scottish right wing. The age of the English longbow may have been

> *In this battayle the Scottes had many great advantages That is to wit the hygh hylles and mountaynes A great wynde with them and soddayne rayne all Contrary to our bowes and archers.* Trewe Encountre, sixteenth century

drawing to a close, but for centuries its range, accuracy and rate of fire was unsurpassed by the infantry weapons which replaced it.

Not halted by the barrage of shot and arrows and crossing the best of the ground on the Scottish left, the vanguard of Home and Huntly was able to remain in good order as it made contact with Edmund Howard's battle, grouped to the south-west of Piper's Hill.

King James's adoption of the Swiss military method seemed to have been vindicated. The packed Scottish echelon formation with its hundreds of levelled pikes was like a spiked juggernaut, its unbroken momentum relentlessly carrying it forward over any in the English front ranks who stood in its way. Most of them ran, pursued by Scottish clansmen at last unshackled from the chafing discipline of their steady advance to battle.

Yet Edmund Howard, youngest son of the Earl of Surrey and in command on the English right wing, stayed to fight on. Battered three times to the ground and his standard-bearer cut to pieces, he still refused to yield. It was a crucial moment for him and his brother, who led the central English division on the slopes of Piper's Hill. Much of Howard's command had scattered into the fields and the Lord Admiral's battle, preoccupied with the enemy to their front, was now at the mercy of Home's no doubt buoyant echelon. But Lord Dacre, stationed at the rear of the English line, spurred his horsemen forward to plug the gap. With no enemy to their front, the successful Scottish battle group had probably slackened their formation, enabling Dacre's border cavalry to wheel and cut through their ranks, snatching Edmund Howard to safety and fighting the Scotsmen to a standstill.

In any event, it is usually claimed that Home had no intention to make any further progress. His soldiers had undoubtedly acquitted themselves well in the early stages but after tussling with the English rearguard made no further contribution to the battle apart from allegedly pillaging the camps of both sides. The criticism they have subsequently received from some quarters has been shared by their leader. Whether Lord Alexander Home's reputed comment at Flodden was that of a callous traitor or not, he was executed three years later

> *He does well that does for himself; we have fought our vanguard already and won … therefore let the rest do their part as we.* Historie and Chronicles of Scotland, sixteenth century

and has been reviled for refusing to aid the Scottish king in his final struggle.

Home may have had other reasons not to interfere. Away to his right the remainder of the Scottish army was encountering as much difficulty with the terrain of Branxton Hill as with their English foes.

On their descent of Branxton Hill, King James's second and third echelons strove not just to maintain their order and dress their lines, but to stay on their feet. They slithered across the rain-soaked surface, many discarding their footwear in an attempt to get a surer grip. At the bottom of the hill their plight worsened. In the valley and unseen to most bar the foremost Scottish ranks lay a seemingly slight ditch which finally shattered the faltering rhythm of their advance and dislocated their hitherto close formation.

Flodden Field has barely changed since 1513. On close inspection today, it

After negotiating the ditch, the Scots faced an uphill slog before they came to 'handestrokes.' (Piper's Hill and monument, position of the Lord Admiral's English banners, can be seen on the horizon to the right of the hedge.)

is easily appreciated why this ditch was such a troublesome obstacle. Narrow but deep and partially filled with stagnant water, the marshy fissure bisects a major tract of the battlefield. It was a mantrap for the Scots and an unexpected place for James's battle plan to stumble towards disaster. Compounding the problem for the Scots, it is also apparent that the slope at the bottom of Branxton Hill becomes deceptively steep. This would have unbalanced the Scots even more and tipped them faster towards the muddy valley floor. As the Scottish echelons slowed and jostled to pick their way across, on the slope above them the English waited.

> *The said Scots were so plainly determyned to abide batail and not to flee, that they put frome thayme thair horses and also put off their boitte and shois.* Trewe Encountre, sixteenth century

Maintaining battle order and the tempo of attack regardless of setbacks was vital to the success of the 'Almeyns manner'. With the advantage of relatively level ground Home's victorious first echelon had shown what could be achieved. But in the congested centre of the battlefield the irritated Scots had neither the depth of training nor the ruthless discipline necessary to regain their order before mounting an attack. Brave determination was not lacking, however, and after they dragged themselves through the clogging wetland they had lost no resolve to come to grips with an enemy they could now clearly see.

And as the first lines of pikes shivered against the Lord Admiral's battle all seemed well for the Scots. The English buckled and bent back. But they did not break. The Scottish second battle division of Lords Crawford, Errol and Montrose, lacking the concerted mass of a properly formed echelon, were slowed and brought to a halt. Behind them, King James's 9,000 strong 'great battle' composed of 'bishops, earls, lords, knights of the realm with many of the commons', had still not come to blows. Against the advice of his nobles King James led his men from the front and it is chronicled that he went into battle as a 'mean soldier'. He shared his troops' frustration and delay in crossing the bog and, expressing further solidarity with the rank and file, he may even have shouldered a pike. If so, he would presently experience its fatal weakness at first hand.

Even handling the levelled pike efficiently would have been a difficult feat to master for largely inexperienced Scottish levies. Their final uphill advance would have been made even more tiring by the handling of such a lengthy weapon with its flexing ash stave. Nevertheless, like the second echelon on his left, James kept order as best he could to finally push against the line of the English commander-in-chief.

But once again the momentum of the Scottish attack was not enough. Surrey's long but shallow battle front was able to cushion his opponent's weakly delivered assault. Across the width of the battlefield, both Scottish echelons had ground to a stop and both armies meshed together, a grinding tangle of bill and pike blades.

> *The thirde batayle of wherin was the kynge of Scottes and moste parte of the noble men of his realm came fyercly upon sayd lord of Surrey.* Trewe Encountre, sixteenth century

Each English battle had stretched backward to hold the Scots but the typically elongated English formation enabled them to wrap around the exposed Scottish flanks. Unable to advance, the Scots pikemen could only clumsily jab their weapons forward, their stalled front lines slashing out wildly but largely without effect. Ominously for the Scots, English men-at-arms and billmen then began to step into the openings the Scots had left between their ranks. In their hurry to engage the enemy the Scots had exposed themselves to counterattack and the English infantry had room to manoeuvre.

The eight-inch spear point of the Scottish pike was mounted on an eighteen-foot-long shaft usually protected from sword cuts by iron sheaths or 'langets'. At Flodden Field it seems these devices did not extend far enough. With a deft swing of their shorter and heavier weapon, the English billmen, out of range of the lunging pikes, began to slice off the ash shafts before moving in for the kill. At a stroke, what had been the leading edge of weapon technology for the Scots had became a dangerous liability. Indeed, seeing the pike's uselessness in close combat, many Scotsmen immediately threw the weapon down and drew their 'great and sharp swords'. But even this did not save them. They were always outreached by the eight-foot

> *The bylles dyd bete and hewe them downe.* Trewe Encountre, sixteenth century

billhook, its vicious curving edge powerful enough to overbalance and club an armoured man to the ground before its stabbing point sought out his weakest points at throat and groin. Almost as if they were harvesting corn the English billmen grimly scythed through the Scottish ranks. Wielding their crude weapons, common English soldiers were slaughtering the finely armoured Scottish nobility.

Silence fell over the battlefield as the afternoon light began to wane. In the grim struggle to survive the Scots had little energy to spare for their characteristic war cries. Much of the fighting was concentrated in the more heavily armoured front lines of the Scottish battles where the noble 'flower' of Scotland were steadily being cut down. To their rear the more poorly equipped levies had little desire to share in their masters' fate. Their feudal duty done, many of them began to slip away, giving the English billmen extra leeway to work in. Evidence also suggests that English archers then began to rejoin the fray, at liberty now to pick off prominent Scottish targets with their bows or to grapple with an already assailed enemy. But even as they began to be outnumbered and surrounded, the remaining Scotsmen fought on with even greater ferocity:

> *And when theyr speres fayled and were spent then they fought with great and sharp swords making lytell or no noys.* Trewe Encountre, sixteenth century

> *It is not to be doubted but the Scottes fought manly and were determyned either to wynne the fylde or to dye.* Trewe Encounter, sixteenth century

At the battle of Flodden Field, many Scotsmen who remained to fight through its closing stages did die. With extraordinary savagery reminiscent of the recent Wars of the Roses, the English army, steadily gaining the upper hand, extended little mercy to their flagging opponents and according to the Bishop of Durham, Thomas Ruthal, 'rid all that came to hand.' For many English soldiers, half-crazed with hunger and the blood heat of battle, ransom became less a priority than annihilating an enemy who had caused them so much hardship.

Yet King James IV of Scotland still lived and fought on within a protective knot of his retainers. In a final desperate attempt to turn the battle in his favour he launched himself towards the red and gold battle standard of the Earl of Surrey. Cutting and stabbing with broadsword and dirk, James disappeared under the billhook strokes. No one saw him fall as the English closed in to tear down the last Scottish colours.

The Scotsmen who might have saved their king stood passively on the eastern edge of Branxton Hill. Argument has been heated concerning the role of the Earls of Lennox and Argyll, who with a battle formation of perhaps 6,000 Highlanders at their disposal were inactive throughout the battle, seemingly oblivious to the predicament of their companions. The earls may have lacked any order to do otherwise, but more likely, because the Highland division was the most scantily armoured of all, it had been assigned the less onerous duty of protecting the Scottish artillery. Lennox and Argyll were finally pricked into action not by the plight of King James, but by a sudden fall of English arrows amongst the ranks of their clansmen.

Belatedly, Sir Edward Stanley had reached the field to lead a double-pronged assault preceded by a devastating longbow volley into Argyll's plaid-wearing troops. A crushing follow up by Stanley's pikemen finished the briefest of skirmishes. Only the bravest Scotsmen, including Lennox and

Argyll, remained to die. The remainder joined a general Scottish rout, radiating out from Branxton, beginning a chase which according to the English Lord Admiral, 'continued three miles with marvellous slaughter.' Meanwhile, across the now darkened battlefield, scavengers were already picking amongst the dead.

Because they were uncertain that all the Scots had fled, many exhausted Englishmen remained at arms through the night. Their precautions proved necessary. At first light, in an unexpected epilogue to the battle, a party of Scottish horsemen made an audacious attempt to retrieve their captured artillery. Hundreds of them, probably led by Lord Home, galloped furiously towards a company of the Lord Admiral's men but were humiliatingly put to flight by sharp fire, said to have been from their own guns. The last Scotsman had been driven from Branxton and for the English, victory was theirs.

Its magnitude was easily gauged. In all directions lay heaped Scottish corpses, possibly numbering 8,000, many of them stripped naked. Pulled from their midst, gruesomely mutilated by arrow and billhook wounds was the body of James IV. Although some of his traumatised subjects refused to accept the bitter reality of it, Scotland's 'noble rose' was dead and his splendid army smashed. With a risky yet inspired tactical march, the Earl of Surrey had wrested the initiative away from the Scottish king. James had been drawn into an unplanned move which dragged his army into the muddy pitfalls of an unknown terrain. When battle came the Scots relied heavily on a single weapon in what was for them an innovative echelon attack. While intrinsically sound, this

> *The Flowers o' the Forest, that fought aye the foremost the prime of our land, lie cauld in the clay.* Jean Elliot, eighteenth century

combat formation required to be well drilled and supplemented by auxiliary infantry to ensure its overall success. Unlimited Scottish courage could not compensate for such deficiencies and the English response was fierce as they hacked down the pikes and the Scotsmen who carried them.

In a few hours on Flodden Field, Scotland lost almost a whole generation of its ruling elite. Yet within a few months the country was again on a war footing. Initially, the surviving nobility talked loudly of an avenging war with England but instead began to scramble for a share in the power behind their new infant king's throne. In 1523 a sizeable Scottish army paused at the Tweed but then, haunted by the memory of Flodden, many of them turned back as the English approached.

Towards the end of his reign, Henry VIII reinstated the hoary claim of sovereignty over Scotland, hoping first to weld the countries together by dynastic marriage but keeping the threat of military subjugation close at hand. Threat became reality with a major English invasion. Henry's 'Rough Wooing' of Scotland was rough indeed. It began in 1544 and this time the North was a transit camp and not a battleground for the troops who instead battered at Scottish towns. After mustering at Newcastle in September 1547, an army led by Protector of the Realm Lord Somerset devastated the Scottish schiltrons at Pinkie Cleugh in Musselburgh. In a 'Black Saturday' of disaster as great as

The memorial on Piper's Hill to the dead of both nations. (Branxton Church in the background.)

Following its capture on the battlefield at Flodden, King James's highly prized Scottish ordnance was taken to Etal Castle. Two eighteenth-century English naval guns now stand at the gate.

Flodden, the Scots, keeping faith with pike formations, were cut to pieces not by the English billhook but by the raking fire of their artillery.

The final major battle in this renewed national savagery was over. With French aid the defeated Scots hit back at English occupation and by 1549 had secured a tremulous peace. But the tradition of mischief at the border had much longer to run. In 1575, on the windswept edge of Northumberland, men from both sides of the divide clashed once more, in a battle that while minor compared to Pinkie, might have toppled the nations back into outright war.

> *With jack and spear and bows all bent,*
> *And warlike weapons at their will.* Traditional Border Ballad

At 1,370 feet above sea level, Carter Bar is rarely a comfortable place to linger. To paraphrase the observation of an old traveller, it is a place where 'even the devil would need to be tethered.' On 7 July 1575, however, this bleak ridge, formerly known as the Reidswire, was deemed a suitable spot for border justice to be seen to be done.

The Vicar's Pele at Corbridge, constructed in the fourteenth century, is a fine example of the characteristic Northumbrian tower house. Such defensive architecture, able to accommodate men and their livestock, was crucial for life on a border at war.

Following the 1549 agreement at Boulogne, the respective government authorities had resumed their efforts to bring their unsettled border populations to heel. It was an invidious task. These were frontier people, their restless lives shaped by centuries of almost incessant war between England and Scotland. Many of them lived by their wits and from the proceeds of their moonlight border raids. In times of war the authorities encouraged cross-border strikes to 'lift' enemy cattle and goods, and in times of relative peace the Wardens appointed to stop them occasionally colluded in the activities of the reiving clans.

This element of banditry ran deeply across the northern line. Yet from it was bred a fighting man whose qualities were in demand from the armies of both nations. Mounted on wiry fleet-footed horses known as 'Hobblers', the Borderers deserved their reputation as fearsome light cavalry and were drafted into both armies to act as scouts or 'prickers'. Protected by 'steel bonnets', the 'jack', a tough padded waistcoat usually reinforced with iron plates, and armed with lance, dagger and bow, the border cavalrymen were fast moving and hard hitting. In battle, however, their loyalty could be suspect. As commanders on both sides had experienced, border horsemen often favoured kin before country if their clansmen appeared in the opposing ranks. Nevertheless they fought with distinction in many battles and at Solway Moss in 1542 for example, although hopelessly outnumbered, their terrier-like attacks turned back an entire Scottish army.

> ... the boldest men, and the hottest, that ever I saw.
> Thomas Howard, Earl of Surrey, 1474–1554

Men such as these rode to the Reidswire in July 1575. It was a day of Truce which ended in bloodshed. Arising from the original Laws of the Marches in 1249, these days or 'diets' gave a formal hearing to the copious grievances of the belligerent border factions. As open air courts they were scheduled to meet monthly but the political climate as well as the weather was often used as an excuse for cancellation by their presiding Wardens.

'Old' Sir John Forster was the greatly experienced Warden of the English Middle March, the administrative district which sprawled over Northumberland from the Cheviots to the Tyne. To survive his weighty responsibilities throughout a career spanning thirty-five years required skilled diplomacy and native cunning in equal measure. In all likelihood his lengthy tenure had also relied upon the complicity and sharp practice of which he was often accused but which was never proven against him. Border defence was his primary duty but peacemaking also demanded his attention. The day of Truce which Forster arranged was at least a line of communication with his almost ungovernable border clans.

Like Wark, Carham and Coldstream, the Reidswire was a customary border location to host any day of Truce. But Forster approached this desolate meeting place with caution for it was also customary for both parties to draw up *en masse* and fully armed. After assurances to obey the conditions of Truce had been given, however, formal proceedings began. All appeared to run smoothly until under a 'bill of complaint' introduced by Sir John Carmichael, Keeper of Liddesdale, the surrender of a notorious English villain named

MR E PARKER,
1 BRINKBURN AVE,
REGENT FARM ESTATE,
GOSFORTH,
NEWCASTLE UPON
TYNE,
NE3, 3HU

bt.com at a later date.

ice - what BT charges for.

os a fault, our engineer can visit. If the fault is due to
ring, you will be charged for the visit. If the fault is with
ot be charged. (Remember: If you rent your line from
ny, please report any faults to them.) When we install a phone
n as a line box. Our network ends at the line box.

ets for an additional charge. (Any wiring or sockets
d for the guarantee period only.) Alternatively you can add
sion wiring and sockets but any wiring or sockets not
n part of our network and they are not covered under our
omer Service Guarantee Scheme. So if this part of your
ental phones) develops a fault, you will be charged for an
. For simple ways to identify and solve faults without a
sult your phone book or www.bt.com/faults

Reidswire Fray 1575: the memorial at Carter Bar to a last spasm of border war.

Farnstein was required. Forster could not comply and an accusation was made, probably impugning the impartiality he was expected to observe. The raised voices of the officials carried to their restive followers and arrows rather than recriminations began to fly.

The Reidswire incident sharply defines the incendiary nature of border life, where the spark always ready to ignite it existed within the prickly border tribesman himself. His easily offended pride would not tolerate insult or even perceived slight. Blood feud could follow from the violence which flared, diligently and murderously pursued for generations after its cause was forgotten.

At the Reidswire it is not certain who made the first bowshot, but all semblance of order was gone and clansmen began to fall into the heather. Forster and Carmichael's attempts to restore control were in vain as Scots reinforcements arrived to give their comrades the upper hand. Fierce fighting mocked the concept of Truce and the English deputy Warden, Sir George Heron, was killed. His side came off the worse and several prominent English officers were captured including Lord Francis Russell, son-in-law of the Warden, and the septuagenarian Forster himself.

During the preceding decades, the authorities had wrung their hands in despair at reports of such misbehaviour by their far-off subjects, some of whom were said by the English Warden Sir John Wharton in 1548 to 'desire continual war for their private gain.' His succinct analysis was just as true in 1575, but the Reidswire fray of that year was quietly overlooked by the Elizabethan government. After a period of renewed turmoil for the North, with a Franco-Scottish expedition into north Northumberland followed by the

England and Scotland at Reidswire ridge: a prospect of peace after the Union of the Crowns?

failed rebellion of the northern earls, this comparatively minor border spat would not be allowed to spoil the 'better peace between the realms' which Queen Elizabeth herself rosily alluded to.

In the aftermath of Reidswire, Scotland was also not disposed to a retaliatory war and Warden John Forster was soon returned to English soil. But border lawbreaking rampaged on and indeed worsened at the century's end. At the Union of the Crowns in 1603, however, a concentrated onslaught began against the reiving culture. Under the clampdown instigated by James I, 'Jeddart Justice' was applied with a vengeance which filled gallows across the border Marches. Execution and exile broke up the armed bands of marauders and never again would such large parties of horsemen thunder across the Reidswire. They have been replaced by a stream of traffic loudly grinding along the modern border highway. But not far away from the border viewing point with its flags of both nations stretched together by the perpetual breeze, all becomes quiet and remote once more. Not easily seen amongst the tufted upland grass is a squat commemorative slab. It recalls the Reidswire as one of the final 'babbles' of a long drawn out border war.

Chapter 9

GOD, KING AND COUNTRY

1603–1644

War between England and Scotland did not end when they were ruled by one king. Less than forty years after the Union of the Crowns, a Scottish army almost as large as that destroyed on Flodden Field was encamped to the west of Newcastle. Their intention was clear. Outside the tent of each Scottish commander was a banner emblazoned in gold with the legend 'For Christ's Crown and Covenant'. The meddling of a stubborn king who was never shaken from the conviction that he answered for his actions 'to God alone' had brought the battle flag of a Scottish holy war to Northumberland.

Resentment against the policies of King Charles I had been growing in England since his dissolution of Parliament in 1628. Resentment of Charles's interference in its religious affairs erupted into riots in Scotland and gun fire at Newburn Ford. This was the 'Bishops' War', a precursor of greater conflict to come.

Predictably, attempts by Archbishop of Canterbury William Laud to impose the Anglican Book of Common Prayer on the Church of Scotland were not well received. Its reading in Edinburgh caused uproar and by early 1638 many Lowland Scots had defiantly signed the National Covenant, declaring their implacable opposition to liturgical reform.

An enraged Charles could not ignore the challenge to his authority posed by the Covenanters and although starved of money as always, scraped together an army to march north. Ahead of him in May 1639 as part of a three-pronged assault, the Marquis of Hamilton reached the Firth of Forth with 5,000 ill-trained Englishmen and a fleet of twenty-eight ships. Fighting seemed inevitable until the English backed off, deterred by a large and well-equipped Scottish army which confronted them at Duns. The Scots had reservations too. Suddenly intimidated by the implications of fighting their monarch, they entered negotiations instead. From the beginning they had been clear that their argument was not with the king but with a devilish league of 'Papists, Atheists and Armenians' who, they believed, misled him. Few observers could have held any illusions about the patchwork treaty which followed, however. Signed on 18 June, the 'Pacification of Berwick' only postponed the major conflict soon to follow.

To strengthen his army and bring his Scottish subjects to heel, Charles was reluctantly obliged to recall the House of Commons. This 'Short Parliament' issued no funds, presented him with a growing list of grievances and was dissolved acrimoniously after three weeks. The loans and direct taxation which he then resorted to only served to heap further criticism upon Charles. Far worse, the pistols which these funds procured for his largely conscripted army of misfits were condemned by Lord Conway in Newcastle as 'patched up' and 'unserviceable'. It was an ominous sign of difficulties to come and foreshadowed the problems with resources which dogged King Charles throughout his subsequent campaigns.

Conway arrived in Newcastle on 22 April 1640. As commander of the garrison he was responsible for assessing the town's worth as a citadel against the Scots, as well as leading an army to oppose them. Within a few months, though, his guarded optimism about the security of Newcastle had turned to despair. At the beginning of August he was convinced that there was 'no hope for this town, but that it will be lost'. His foreboding was induced by the continuing vulnerability of Newcastle to an expected artillery bombardment, particularly on its southern flank where it was overlooked by Gateshead's riverside hills. Yet more than this, he was dismayed by the calibre and conduct of the men serving under him. A mutiny was brewing amongst them which deductions from their meagre allowance to pay for repairs to their shoddy equipment was unlikely to forestall. Their protests met with harsh military discipline. To nip this rebellion in the bud an example was to be made amongst the ranks. According to Lord Conway it was intended 'to terrify the rest'. With what he probably believed was a compassionate gesture, Conway pardoned one of the pair of ringleaders he had condemned to death. But they were compelled to throw dice to decide who would be shot in Newcastle's Bigg Market.

> I have been around the walls of the town, which are in many places very high, and it will be ill scaling them, but in other places they are better to be attempted. Lord Conway, April 1640

The Scots cast the dice for a different purpose. A Scottish force led by hardened veterans of continental wars had been massing near the border since early July. Their commander, Sir Alexander Leslie, appointed after distinguished service as Field Marshal to King Gustav Adolphus in Sweden, gave the order to ford the Tweed near Coldstream. On the late afternoon of 20 August, after tossing dice across a drumhead to decide who would have the honour, James, Earl of Montrose led the Scottish vanguard into a woefully undefended Northumberland.

Newcastle Town Walls, 'in many places very high'. Substantial remains of the West Walls, viewed towards Morden Tower, which was built about 1280.

Village church bells in England were allegedly chiming midnight as the Scottish rearguard finally emerged from the river. Henry Bowett, an Englishman describing himself as 'being disguised', claimed to have seen

> *... about 300 tents pitched besides small coults, 32,000 men armed, besides sutlers, 1,000 waggons together with carriages drawne with six or eight little oxen and two or four little horses laden with provisions. 23 Regeints [regiments], some of eight, others of ten or twelve and two of fifteen coleurs. Seventy lessor pieces for the field, seventy two or seventy three troupe of horses, but they told me 5,000 in all, but I could not believe them. 600 head of cattelle, 4,000 sheep, 3,000 women.*

Despite folk memories and contemporary exaggeration there is no doubt that Leslie moved south with a large and comparatively well-equipped force. They appear to have been largely disciplined and self-sufficient, paying for supplies instead of stealing them and generally not submitting the Northumberland countryside to the destruction wrought by so many of their predecessors. Latest research estimates their main body to have consisted of 19,000 men in pike and musket divisions, at least six times greater than the English infantry fielded to stop them. Greater in cavalry strength as well, it was only in heavy artillery that the Scots seem to have been at a disadvantage. Nevertheless, strapped to horses and packed into carts were a wide range of light field pieces, whose manoeuvrability and fire power were to cut a swathe

A practical if ugly bridge, built in 1893, now straddles the Tyne at Newburn. It occupies the site of the ancient ford and faces the Norman church tower as the English army did in August 1640.

through the brittle English ranks at Newburn Ford.

In three dense columns and with ten miles between each, the Scottish army marched south along the Devil's Causeway, knots of blue ribbon decorating the Lowland bonnets worn by every rank to proclaim their support for the Covenant. In Newcastle, Conway's disquiet continued. Close by were the fords around Newburn village, one which it was said could be crossed by a child. Through time immemorial they had been used by invading Scottish armies. When Leslie's army drew nearer to Eachwick, barely more than a day's march away to the north-west, it was highly likely that the Scots were about to use them once more. Conway's despatches to King Charles's headquarters at York became almost desperate in tone, as it seemed to him that his worst fears were about to be realised:

> *If they have a mind to take Newcastle, should they come to Gateside, they may do it very quickly.* Lord Conway to Secretary Vane, 25 August 1640

Frantic activity commenced at Newburn. An English regiment already in place to guard the ford began instead to excavate its approaches. Under the direction of a chief engineer from Newcastle, three earthwork forts or 'sconces' were hurriedly thrown up on the Tyne's southern bank. They covered a broad stretch of river from Ryton Willows in the west to Stella Haugh in the east and each of them was manned with English cannon and musketeers. But the infantrymen took little consolation as they looked across from the gun emplacements to the familiar Norman tower of Newburn's parish church. Concealed by a line of small hills to the north, the Scots army rumbled nearer as one English soldier prophetically complained of 'our miserable works in the valley, where we lay so exposed'.

Yet even at this eleventh hour Conway still wavered, suspicious that the Scottish descent towards the fords may have been a feint. On Friday 28 October, at Conway's headquarters at Stella Hall, a grand Elizabethan house on the heights to the south of Newburn, the possibility of English withdrawal in the face of superior Scottish force was discussed. But Lord Conway's mind was made up for him. The decision to stand and fight at the Tyne was taken by the English high command at York. Patience exhausted, the Earl of Strafford issued a peremptory despatch to his unadventurous northern field commander ordering him to 'fight with them' during any attempted river passage by the Scots:

Admit me to deal plainly with you. I find all men in this place extream ill satisfied with the guiding of our Horse, and publish it infinitely to your disadvantage, that having with you one thousand Horse and five hundred foot, you should suffer an enemy to march so long a way without one skirmish, nay without once looking upon him. And it imports you most extreamly, by some Noble action, to put yourself from under the weight of ill tongues. Lord Strafford to Conway, 27 August 1640

While Conway digested this stinging rebuke, the Scottish army was taking advantage of the plentiful cover available to them in an abandoned Newburn village. Behind walls and hedges and the thick scrub and gorse which then encrusted the riverbanks, they took up their firing positions. The opportunity for Conway's redemption was at hand but the action his inadequate army took to achieve it was far from noble.

A single musket shot rang out to begin the Battle of Newburn Ford. Throughout a bright Friday morning of 28 August, both armies nervously watched as the tide ebbed across the gleaming flood plain of the River Tyne. A reassurance by Leslie that his mission sought only religious freedom and wished to present a petition to King Charles was politely rebuffed by Conway. Shortly after midday, as the ford level dropped, a Scottish officer rode out to water his horse. Perhaps his interest in the English fortifications 250 yards from him across the Tyne proved to be his undoing. Or perhaps the ostentatiously plumed headgear he was said to have been wearing tempted a sharp-eyed English gunner to try his luck. Trained snipers using weapons with rifled gun barrels were rarely found amongst English armies of this period. It is therefore likely that the unfortunate Scotsman was brought down by a chance shot from the infamously inaccurate musket fired at its maximum range. Yet a contemporary military theorist believed that organised musketry could send 'the messengers of death'. It would send many more as the afternoon drew on.

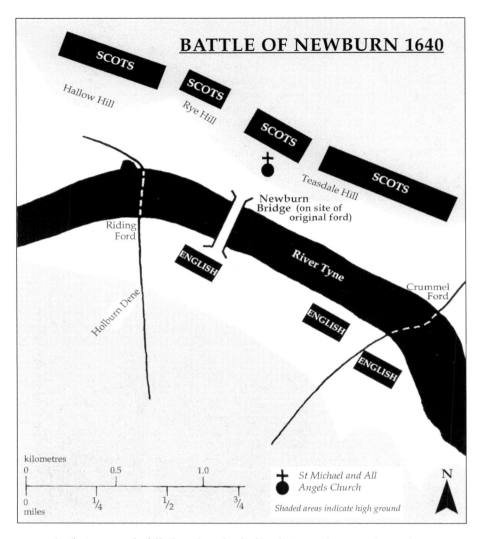

BATTLE OF NEWBURN 1640

SCOTS

SCOTS

SCOTS

SCOTS

Hallow Hill

Rye Hill

Teasdale Hill

Newburn
Bridge (on site of
original ford)

Riding
Ford

ENGLISH

River Tyne

Crummel
Ford

ENGLISH

Holburn Dene

ENGLISH

kilometres
0   0.5   1.0

0   ¼   ½   ¾
miles

*St Michael and All
Angels Church*

Shaded areas indicate high ground

N

As their comrade fell, three hundred of Leslie's cavalrymen plunged across the ford but were repulsed by a volley of close-range musket fire which crashed from the primary English redoubt. Soon the riverside was wreathed in gun smoke as the opposing batteries opened up. Newburn was described to be 'ablaze' and the noise must have been deafening, rolling downstream like thunder to warn Newcastle that its future was being decided.

Improvements in artillery technology in the century since Flodden had been minimal. But as that battle showed, field placement of guns and their flexibility could have a crucial bearing on their performance. Leslie must have welcomed the English abandonment of the high ground at Newburn and capped Hallow, Rye and Teasdale hills with his heaviest cannon. Others were unlimbered in front of the Church of St Michael and smaller weapons were even hauled to the top of its tower. For closer-range work the Scots were also equipped with about eighty 'frams', also called Swedish pieces or leather guns, fascinating ordnance which were described by a later historian as 'temporary cannon manufactured at Edinburgh of tin for the bore, with a coating of leather, all secured by tight cordage, two of which a horse could carry'. Although only

> *The Scots, having the advantage of the rising ground above Newborne, easily discerned the posture and motion of the English army in the valley on the south side of the river; but the posture of the Scots army the English could not discern.* John Rushforth, 1640

capable of about a dozen discharges, these lightweight pieces of improvised artillery could be speedily assembled and transferred around the battlefield.

The tower of Newburn St Michael's provided a steady platform for lighter Scottish field artillery.

Seventeenth-century cannon fire was observed by a contemporary to 'frighten more than it hurts.' As the Scots bombardment intensified at Newburn, however, both effects appear to have been achieved in equal measure. Scottish fire power began to take its toll. Turf-covered English breastworks were particularly vulnerable to plunging fire from the more highly elevated Scottish cannon. As their heavy round shot, weighing up to fifty pounds, fell into the emplacements, English soldiers and their flimsy morale were torn to shreds. Scottish firing seems to have been concentrated upon the primary English sconce commanded by Colonel Lunsford. Initial hits had killed many of its occupants and further strikes ended its resistance. Lunsford's desperate pleas could not rally English soldiers who, complaining about the lack of expected reinforcements, 'threw down their arms and would abide in the fort no longer.' Detonating the gunpowder stores, they began to scurry back across the fields, trying to escape from the missiles which plummeted down around them. Later, partly to deflect criticism of his own leadership, Conway described his disorderly infantry as 'the meanest sort of men about London', but perhaps no more could have been expected from raw recruits placed into the mouth of enemy cannon. Conway's judgement of the cavalry who then charged against the Scots at Newburn was just as defeatist.

Following the elimination of the largest English fort, the ford lay open to the Scots and a small body of horse from Leslie's College of Justice Regiment tentatively moved across. Lord Wilmot, in command of the English cavalry force, galloped from Stella Haugh to meet them and drove them back into the river. Only under heavy Scottish fire did Wilmot retreat as the Scots regrouped for a decisive assault. Their guns had levelled the secondary English fort and now only the English cavalry could block their way.

At about four o'clock in the afternoon, with the ford at its lowest, the Scottish vanguard at last crossed the Tyne. Two regiments of Scots foot led by Lords Louden and Lindsay were shepherded over by a cavalry contingent. As they reached the Durham shore, they were counterattacked by the English horse, funnelling out towards them from a gap between thick hedgerows. Lord Wilmot spurred twelve Cavalier squadrons forward. Many amongst them were the county gentry and their retainers, accomplished horsemen who would form the backbone of Royalist forces during the early years of the Civil War to come.

In the thrashing melee of horses and men that followed around the water meadows of Ryton, no one would give way. Wilmot and his men fought on until a Royal Standard of Lord Conway's own troop was captured and its bearer shot dead. By then the main Scots infantry, clear of the river, was massing against them. A crackling broadside of musketry emptied English saddles and was enough of a warning for any English foot who remained to witness it. They joined their fellows in a general rout, ascending east and west on the valley slope, scrambling up Peth Lane and Holborn Dene to seek sanctuary in the English camps at Ryton and Stella. Wilmot's day of action was not yet over, however, and gathering together the few Englishmen still prepared to fight, he struck at the Scots one last time.

A battered summerhouse is the last vestige of Lord Conway's headquarters at Stella Hall, which was demolished in 1955.

A quarter of a century later, the story of Wilmot's final skirmish at Newburn was written down. Although probably embellished during the intervening years, it conveys well the confusion of mounted combat using pistol and sword. After a failed ambush in woodland above Stella Haugh in which poorly co-ordinated musket fire gave his position away, Wilmot's troop was overwhelmed and he was captured by the Scots. Although his helmet was knocked away in the tussle, 'neither by sword, carbine nor pistol which pell-mell were brandished and discharged at his bare head and came so near his face that it glowed with the heat of fire issuing from them was he either hurt or touched.' Only Wilmot and his cavalry emerged with some pride from the English debacle at Newburn, appearing to be far from the cowards that Conway branded them.

Examples of the wide range of ammunition discovered at Newburn.

With the English infantry in full flight, their faint-hearted defence of Newburn Ford was over. Mercifully, Leslie's order for restraint was obeyed and there was no vengeful pursuit by the Scottish victors. In contrast with so many other purportedly religious conflicts, slaughter of the ungodly losers did not conclude the fighting and at Newburn overall fatalities seem to have been comparatively few. From the evidence of a burial pit uncovered to the east of the church during quarrying in 1897, the dead in this second Bishops' War have been estimated to be 300 on each side.

In the dawn after the fall of Newburn, Conway abandoned Newcastle and its cache of arms and provisions to the waiting Scots. He retreated towards Durham, jettisoning artillery pieces into the Tyne and still bemoaning that his army was 'unprovided of all necessaries'. After some hesitation Newcastle embraced its fate and a bareheaded mayor ushered General Leslie across the bridge from Gateshead to be entertained at a banquet in his honour. But four years later when the same Scottish 'old, little, crooked souldier' returned to the walls of Newcastle, he received a less cordial welcome.

Considering the legacy of aggression between them, it was ironic that in 1640 the Scots occupied a North of England they had laid no territorial claim to. After the token Royalist resistance at Newburn Ford had been swept aside, all six northern counties were in Scottish hands and by the Treaty of Ripon on 21 October 1640, to the chagrin of King Charles, they were paid to exercise their control. To raise the vast ransom required to end this humiliating occupation Charles was forced to recall Parliament and plunge again into a bitter argument which deepened division and ended in war.

For Northumberland and Durham, Scottish rule and the crippling taxation levied to fund it caused widespread depopulation and economic ruin. Many lives were seriously affected, particularly those dependent on a burgeoning coal trade which was badly disrupted by the year-long Scottish occupation. A considerably poorer Newcastle was finally set free in August 1641 to be given the briefest respite. One year later, almost to the day, King Charles raised his standard at Nottingham and civil war began.

Newcastle remained a Royalist stronghold, its sympathies encouraged by William Cavendish, Earl of Newcastle, who was appointed as the town's governor shortly before hostilities commenced. One of Charles's staunchest supporters, Cavendish mobilised the local trained bands and fortified Tynemouth and South Shields. Probably acting on earlier recommendations, he also ordered Newcastle's defensive perimeter to be stiffened. In August 1643, Parliament's alliance with Scotland gave added urgency to the builders' toil. Walls were repaired, gun emplacements were let into them and two independent forts were built at Shieldfield on the east and at Carr's Battery overlooking the river shore. Shieldfield in particular, 'within half musket shot of the town walls', would be invaluable in the protracted siege of Newcastle to come.

With an army of 20,000 men, Andrew Leslie, now Earl of Leven, crossed a frozen River Tweed on 15 January 1644. He had received his new title from King Charles but reneged on his promise not to bear arms against him as the

Scots brandished their Covenant again. Alnwick and Morpeth Castles were no hindrance to him and only the 'dismal snowie season' held the Scottish army back.

> *No Covenant whatever can justify your march into the bowels of another kingdom.* Thomas Glemham, January 1644

Sir Thomas Glemham backed respectfully away, unable to match his indignant rhetoric with any action from his puny Royalist force. By midday on 3 February, as the ice began to thaw, the Scottish army drew up to the 'old walled town on the Tyne'. Only a barricaded Newcastle could now prevent their clean sweep across the North.

The reply of Mayor John Marley to the Scottish surrender request could not have been more forthright:

> *... our allegiance to his Majesty, for whose humour and preservation, together with the religion and laws of this kingdom, we intend to hazard our lives and our fortune.* John Marley, 3 February 1644

With a force of perhaps only 1,500 effective combatants, Newcastle would fight Leven rather than repeat the submission of four years before.

Without waiting for the arrival of heavy artillery which was being transported by sea, Leven launched an immediate attack. In what was a foretaste of bitter exchanges to come, Shieldfield's fort was assaulted from east and west by parties of Scottish infantry. According to one of them they stormed towards the fortification 'discharging their muskets very courageously in the midst of the greatest disadvantage that could be, being in the open fields almost fully in the view of the enemy; the enemy being sheltered with fortifications, and answering our musket shots with cannon and muskets.' Fighting continued in the darkness. By midnight a senior Scottish commander was amongst the dead and the suburbs of Newcastle were engulfed with flame. Outside its walls, a 'ring of fire' was lit, not by the Scots, but by Newcastle's defenders who were ordered to sacrifice their homes rather than surrender their town.

Newcastle (from Gateshead's Windmill Hills). Within range of Scottish cannon in 1644.

For some days afterwards the Scottish army mounted no more assaults, but in the words of one of their Colonels still pressed 'close under the verie walls' of Newcastle. Surrounded by a ditch which was over twenty yards wide and six feet deep, this medieval construction remained a forbidding sight. Twelve feet high and eight feet in thickness, the town wall had a circumference of over two miles with gates and ramparts guarded by seventeen towers. In terms of almost biblical grandeur, Scotsman William Lithgow described the sight of them:

> *The walls about the town are both high and strong, built both without and within with saxoquadrato; and maynely fenced with dungeon towres, interlarded also with turrets, and alongst with them a large and defensive*

On the eastern flank of Newcastle's protective walled circuit, Plummer Tower was strengthened with the addition of an artillery bastion during the Civil War.

battlement, having eight sundry ports and four parochial churches, the which walls, the defendants within had marveilously fortified, rampiering them with interlinings and mountagnes of earth. ... The walls here of Newcastle are a great deal stronger than those of Yorke, and not unlike to the walls of Avineon, but especially of Jerusalem. William Lithgow, 1644

After the difficulties of his early attack, Leven, a master of siege warfare, may have held back to gauge the strength of Newcastle's 'old grey walls' or perhaps the weather had become too severe for further direct operations. In the meantime he sealed the entrance to the River Tyne by blockading its forts with vessels from Parliament's fleet of warships. On 19 February the next attack was launched. But it was ordered by the Earl of Newcastle and it came from within the surrounded town.

On 19 February, despite the Scottish clampdown, Royalist cavalry led by Lord Langdale broke out from Newcastle. Riding hard, they surprised and dispersed two Scots horse regiments held in reserve at Corbridge. Although their success was short-lived, their sprightly initiative appeared to have shaken the Scots. After leaving a substantial force and cannon which had been delivered from the nearby port of Blyth, Leven temporarily turned away from Newcastle. His principal destination was Yorkshire where he meant to link with Sir Thomas Fairfax and his Parliamentarian army to squeeze the Royalists between them. But time remained for a Scottish diversion into Durham.

Although a Royal commissioner was rushed north to organise the port's defence, Sunderland, lacking the walled fortifications of its Tyneside neighbour, was taken by the Scots on 4 March. Employing tactics disturbingly familiar to those of much later warfare, they then excavated long sections of trenches. These were dug in the old Pan-Field area of the town and the earth spoil which marked their edges was visible until the early nineteenth century.

But the Earl of Newcastle remained on the offensive, determined that the passage of the Scots through the region would not be comfortable. Reinforced from Durham and Yorkshire, he faced them down in the hedgerow-lined fields and narrow lanes surrounding Sunderland. In heavy snowfall, sporadic and inconsequential contacts appear to have made between the armies. These desultory clashes have since been rather grandiosely dubbed by some historians as 'the Battle of Boldon Hills'. Certainly no full-scale battle took place and the topography of the district does not particularly merit such a description. But the rising ground around Boldon's parish church of St Nicholas would have been eagerly contested by rival commanders. As they still do today, these high and wide meadows provide a superb observation platform. Sunderland harbour lies directly to the east and the approaches to Newcastle can be viewed across the fells to the north-west. The Scots were said by the seventeenth-century English historian John Rushforth to have 'drew up their army in battallia', and both sides peppered each other with musket and cannon fire. But apart from a small Scottish coin found in a ditch near the village of Herrington, no physical trace has emerged of these distant wintry skirmishes.

By spring of 1644, however, more pressing events in Yorkshire precluded any possibility of a major engagement in Durham. Royalists and Parliamentarians left the North to converge on York and fight a conclusive battle. On 2 July at Marston Moor, the aura of invincibility surrounding Prince Rupert, the flamboyant Royalist commander, was lost forever. Arriving late on the battlefield, the Earl of Newcastle's regiment of 'Whitecoat' Northumbrians refuted Rupert's insult that they were 'all drunk' and distinguished themselves in the midst of the Royalist disaster. Their ammunition spent, they refused to surrender and fought to the death with musket butt and pike. The pinned down occupants of Newcastle must have shuddered at the news. After this most decisive Royalist defeat and the subsequent capitulation of York, the Earl of Leven was now free to resume the siege of their town.

You shall ... by all meanes endevor to reduce and secure the towne of Newcastell, Castelle Tynemouth and all other places possessed by the enemy.
Commission of Lord Callender, 9 June 1644

Even before Leven had returned to Newcastle, however, a second Scottish army had arrived to add to its misery. His orders clear, the Earl of Callender and 10,000 men scoured any residual opposition from Durham, leaving Scots garrisons at Stockton and Hartlepool before turning back towards the Royalist salient on the Tyne.

Outside Newcastle a futile attempt was made to check his progress, but William Lithgow, 'an eye witness and observer', claimed that when confronted with the defenders of Newcastle, Callender 'beat them from the hill, chased them down the Gatesyde, and hushing them along the bridge, closed them within the towne.' It would take months of heavy fighting to prise them out.

Five batteries of Scottish cannon were positioned in Gateshead, probably at the east of a series of riverfront slopes known as the Windmill Hills. From there Scottish gunners could direct 'fiery employments' against the walls and towers and beyond into the warren of Newcastle streets. But the Scottish bombardment did not go unanswered. Newcastle's Mayor John Marley ordered artillery to be rolled into the castle compound and onto the 'half moon' fortified tower from where the guns roared out a reply.

With such a wide area of Newcastle beneath the Scottish gun barrels, their bombardment began to take a deadly toll. Civilian casualties were inflicted by stray shot and flying debris and severe damage was caused to the town walls and the buildings it enclosed. Leven returned on 12 August to close the net. Bridging the river with keel boats downstream he crossed with his army and brought more cannon into play.

Yet encircled as they were, Newcastle's defence force was not overawed. With grudging admiration Lithgow speaks of an 'inveterate enemy, making now and then diverse sallies from town' to 'engage themselves into great jeopordies.' Similarly, as the gaps in them widened, Marley was said to have organised makeshift repairs to the town's shattered walls.

Despite the increasingly miserable condition of his town and its inhabitants throughout the summer of 1644, John Marley steadfastly refused demands to surrender by the Scots. It seems that his Royalist principles far outweighed the humanitarian plight of his civilian population. Scottish commissioners, returning empty-handed from negotiations, found the mayor's attitude to be 'very high'. Increasingly exasperated, Leven is subsequently said to have threatened to destroy the steeple of St Nicholas' Church if surrender was not immediate:

> *If it was to fall it should not fall alone; that the same moment he destroyed the beautiful structure, he should bathe his hands in the blood of his countrymen.*
> Henry Bourne, 1736

Rising to 200 feet, the graceful tower of this beautiful landmark, the 'heart and soul of the town', must have presented a tempting target to the Scottish gunners. But it was never disturbed, saved by Marley's ungentlemanly but effective counter-threat to fill its elegant lantern with Scottish prisoners.

Indirectly, the walls of Newcastle were toppled and the siege brought to an end by growing demands to restore the coal trade. With winter approaching and the price of coal increasing sharply, London and its Parliamentary administration was becoming restive. Reports of the siege were eagerly followed in the capital and hopes were raised that 'we may have yet before October be ended a fleet of Newcastle coals.' If this were not enough for Leven, another refusal to surrender accompanied by an impertinent note from Marley was the ultimate provocation.

By this time preparations for the final assault were well advanced. Colliers from Elswick and Benwell had tunnelled beneath the walls to enable mines to be laid. On 20 October, after a morning of particularly ferocious bombardment, the charges were detonated to signal the storming to begin.

By Whitefriars' Tower and Close Gate, Newcastle's defenders staged successive charges to hold the enemy back, but the reinforced Scots regiments began to pour through the breaches. Others clattered scaling ladders against the walls to join their comrades on the other side and push

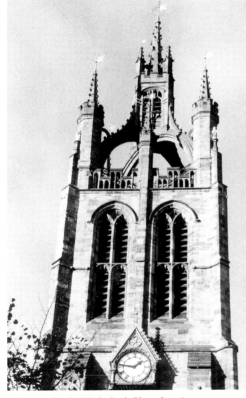

Newcastle, St Nicholas' Church spire. Without doubt its crowning glory but unappreciated by any Scottish prisoners who may have been held there during the siege.

What came to be known as Newcastle's 'Black Gate' (right foreground) was part of a barbican added to the royal castle in 1247 by Henry III. The church of St Nicholas, elements of which date from the twelfth century, became a cathedral in 1881.

their way into the town 'with colours flying and roaring drummes'.

Resistance continued to be stiff, however, as significant towers and thoroughfares were bitterly contested by Newcastle's garrison. As the street fighting moved towards an inevitable conclusion it was pictured in characteristic fashion by Lithgow:

> *The thundering cannon roaring from our batteries without, and theirs rebounding from the castle within; the thousandes of musket balls flyeing at other's faces like to the droving aylestones from septentrion blasts; the clangour and carving of naked and unsheathed swords; the pushing of brangling pykes crying for blood.* William Lithgow, 1644

Despite Lithgow's obvious fondness for colourful excess, there is little doubt that the climax of the siege was ferocious. Its final hours of hard

In the final stage of Newcastle's 1644 siege, a mine was exploded near this section of wall at Hanover Street, and it was breached by Scottish artillery fire.

combat claimed the lives of over one hundred Scottish soldiers and thirty of their officers. No figures are available for Royalist dead, although a more sober account claims that the Scots 'killed very few, after they were entered.' Another official report delivered to London on 29 October refers to Newcastle's defenders who 'played very hotly and desperately from the castle upon the breaches and from the flanking towers of the walls with scattered shot.'

Yet after the Scottish breakthrough, the garrison was steadily overwhelmed. Marley, obdurate to the last, fell back upon prepared positions within the castle compound. For two days he held out in the Norman keep until, running the gauntlet of a starving and disgruntled mob who blamed him solely for their misfortune, he submitted to the Scots.

Within a few days Tynemouth, its garrison severely depleted by plague, followed Newcastle to surrender and Leven controlled all of Northumberland and Durham. With the prospect of the coal embargo being lifted, a citizen of London rejoiced that 'methinks I am warm with the very conceit of Newcastle being taken.' For Charles I, however, the fall of Newcastle and the loss of the North-East was another step closer to the scaffold on a cold January day less than five years later.

Newcastle's loyalty was not forgotten by the Stuarts and is still commemorated in the town's motto: 'She bravely and triumphantly defends.' But without any realistic chance of relief after Marston Moor, the siege of Newcastle could have only one conclusion. Sir John Marley, who escaped from Scottish custody and was eventually to become mayor of Newcastle again, delayed its capitulation for as long as possible. With a motley band of defenders, said to comprise 'but eight hundred of the trained band, and some nine hundred besides of volunteers, prest men, colliers, keillmen, and poore tradesmen', the town of Newcastle had stubbornly resisted the power of a combined Scottish army for almost three months.

Newcastle: keep and cathedral. The Norman keep was Mayor John Marley's last refuge in October 1644. It survived the Scots but was fortunate to escape the enthusiasm of Victorian railway builders who destroyed much else of the castle area.

Tynemouth Castle fell shortly after the surrender of Newcastle in 1644. Four years later, holding out again for King Charles, the rivermouth fort was besieged once more.

Armorial Bearings of the City and County of Newcastle upon Tyne. The shield and castle motif was augmented by a crest and supporting sea-horses in 1575, and acquired its famed motto following the siege in 1644.

As its military significance declined, Heber Tower on Newcastle's West Walls found other uses. By the late nineteenth century it housed a blacksmith's forge.

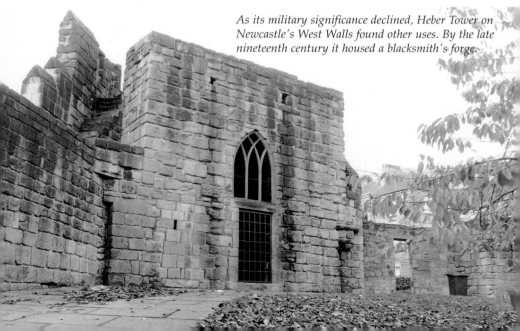

Chapter 10

HOME FRONT
1644–1918

Sir John Marley's last stand at the walls of Newcastle was also the last major battle to be fought in the North-East. No more would great armies clash on its soil. But conflict continued and over the next two centuries rebellion and riot marked the region's painful transition to the modern age. Fears of a Catholic succession led to the ousting of James Stuart from England in 1688. He was replaced by the solidly Protestant William of Orange. During the decades of unrest which followed this 'Glorious Revolution', the dispossessed Jacobites, as the followers of James II, the last Stuart king, came to be known, clung desperately for support to the counties of Northumberland and Durham. It was anticipated that the Catholic gentry of these northern counties, many of them Royalists during the Civil War, would rise in revolt to wear the white Jacobite cockade and welcome their king from exile. But when the opportunity arrived, most of them settled for idealism instead of action.

An early shockwave from England's dynastic upheaval broke on Northumberland's shores. King James had fled to a French welcome at St Germaine which was quickly translated to military backing. In July 1691, a French squadron of eight vessels captained by naval adventurers Jean Bart and Claude Forbin anchored in Druridge Bay off the Northumberland coast. A landing party struck out across the dunes to plunder the village of Widdrington and its hinterland, causing damage that was tallied at £6,000. In 1715 a more expensive and potentially dangerous threat materialised.

Living at the exiled Stuart court in St Germaine was the king's cousin James Radcliffe, who as Earl of Derwentwater was to become the figurehead for the Jacobite cause in Northumberland. In October 1715, after the Stuart banner of rebellion had been raised in Scotland, the young earl set off from his estate at Dilston near Corbridge to gather in his anticipated flock of recruits.

It soon became apparent that disappointingly few were forthcoming. Making matters worse, an argument broke out with the earl's co-conspirator, Northumberland MP Tom Forster, about the leadership of this amateurish band. For days the potential rebels milled around the North, while to the east, the town of Newcastle was given time to make ready. Some remedial work had been carried out on the town wall after its pounding by the Scots in 1644, but evidence suggests that half a century later much remained to be done.

Nevertheless, during October 1715, the magistrates and deputy lieutenants hastily assembled the militia and trained bands and strengthened Newcastle's gates with 'stone and lime'. Regular troops soon marched through them to steady the nerves, although there was no sign of attack from a poorly led enemy already showing signs of collapse. Aware they had wasted their chance to secure Newcastle, the rebels stumbled wearily towards Lancashire where they were surrounded by government troops and rounded up after a brief fight. Yet the Earl of Derwentwater fought determinedly before the Jacobites surrendered in the barricaded streets of Preston.

A sorry affair which had run its course brought death to the earl on Tower Hill and ruin to his family when Dilston was sequestered. Lauded in ballads as Northumberland's own 'bonny lord', the romantic Earl of Derwentwater was brought down by a poorly organised revolt which was starved of northern support. Thirty years later Scotland's 'Bonny Prince' would encounter similar problems.

In 1745, the Young Pretender Charles Edward Stuart, like his ill-fated predecessors, opted for the western and shortest route of rebellion into England. The road through Wooler towards Newcastle was considered by the Jacobites, but dismissed because of heavy winter rain and the threat posed by Berwick's powerful garrison. But had Prince Charlie's depleted ranks of clansmen marched into Northumberland they would have met with precious little enthusiasm. In 1745, to an even greater extent than they had done in the earlier revolt, the Catholic aristocracy of north-east England tightly closed their doors and did not stir to bring about a Stuart restoration. A rowdy northern populace took to the streets and loudly proclaimed their contempt for the 'king across the water':

> From jesuits, friars, and monks in their hoods,
> Who will save our souls, and seize our goods,
> And with fire and faggot will purge all our bloods,
> For ever, good Lord, deliver us. A New Protestant Litany, 2 November 1745

At Derby, on 5 December 1745, the Pretender's hoped for assault on London was rejected by his council chiefs and the rebellion petered out in acrimony and disillusion. The Highlanders began a bitter retreat which ended in near annihilation in the blinding sleet at Culloden.

Before this conclusive victory, the performance of the Hanoverian army had been woefully inadequate. Early in the campaign they had fled from the field at Prestonpans and in January 1746 their discipline again failed; this time

Gateshead House, 'a mansion-house, with a popish chapel within it'. Its ruins were visible long after it was burned down in 1746.

on the outskirts of Falkirk in the face of a surprise enemy attack. Veteran Lieutenant General Henry Hawley paid the price for this added humiliation and was relieved of overall command in favour of the twenty-four-year-old yet battle-hardened Duke of Cumberland, younger son of the Hanoverian English king.

The duke hurried north, reaching Gateshead in the early hours of 28 January. Delayed by the poor condition of the roads, he had abandoned his coach at Durham for a horse lent to him by George Bowes, MP for the town. On finally entering Gateshead, the portly duke and his red-coated dragoon escort were greeted by excited onlookers who clustered around the gardens of Gateshead House, a mansion close to the main street and the derelict chapel of St Edmund. The predominantly loyalist crowd may have congregated there deliberately to intimidate the Catholic owners of the house. At the outset of rebellion the authorities had clamped down on the movements of known Catholics and Jacobite sympathisers. Already mobs had attacked 'papist mass houses' in Sunderland and Newcastle. That some members of the Riddle family who owned Gateshead House had entered the priesthood and that the household was served by Jesuit chaplain John Walsh, almost guaranteed the outbreak of violence which followed.

Many of those straining to glimpse the passing duke were Keelmen, a toughly independent group of riverboat workers with a boisterous reputation. They climbed the walls of Gateshead House for a clearer view and its gardener unwisely unleashed his dogs. High spirits turned to anger as the mob then vented their rage on the 'papist chapel' conveniently at hand.

Lurid flames from the funeral pyre of Gateshead House lit the way to Newcastle for the duke and his companions who cantered past its blazing wreck. It appears that Woodness the gardener and Jesuit chaplain Walsh escaped the inferno. But they would never be able to return. In Gateshead's community of 'good Protestants' no one dared to rebuild the house. Its charred embers, a token of bigotry and persecution, slowly disintegrated in the fields. An expanding industrial town crept up to its ruins in the nineteenth century yet failed to erase every trace of one of Gateshead's earliest and, as hinted at by a rare print, finest buildings. A pilastered Tudor doorway from Gateshead House has survived, probably because of its proximity to the High Street Church of St Edmund's. Sealed into a boundary wall beside the church portico, this door may appear to be nothing more than a salvaged architectural curio or perhaps an enigmatic entrance to nowhere. But forever shut behind it is the ghostly spectre of an uneasy past.

After 1745, religious and national rivalries certainly lived on but Englishmen and Scotsmen, united under one Union flag, increasingly fought together against foreign enemies. Yet eighteenth-century Georgian society continued to be racked by popular unrest in town and countryside. Politicians were openly attacked outside Parliament, bread riots forced magistrates to lower the cost of food and armed bands of poachers roamed at will. And in the North-East, vandalism which had surfaced at Gateshead escalated into bloodshed in the market-place of a Northumberland town.

William Allen was an officer with the North York Militia quartered in Newcastle where he had received orders to march to Hexham and 'put a stop to riotous assemblies to be held there.' With no police force to call on during increasing civil disorder, northern magistrates depended on the deployment of militia bands to provide security. These were usually imported from different regions. Indeed, during the Gordon Riots in 1780, the Northumberland Militia patrolled the streets of London where according to their own official records they 'prudently conducted' live firing against protesters.

> *Arrived safe at Hexham, at ten – found the people all resolute, and determined to rise.* William Allen, 8 March 1761

Militias had long been in existence of course, but in 1757 with increasing domestic unrest and war on three continents, legislation was passed to swell the ranks of England's home defence force. A wide-ranging ballot was introduced which the militant working men of Northumberland said 'none of us will submit to' and it became a focus of further civil disturbance. Jostling mobs had forced suspension of the ballot throughout the North, but on 9 March 1761, the protesting crowd had grown too large and the stakes became too high for the forces of law and order to back down.

> *At nine were under arms – at ten marched to the town hall with the justices took possession of all the avenues leading to the hall, and drew up our men in the market place.* William Allen, 9 March 1761

On that Monday morning in Hexham's market square, crammed between the Abbey and the towering Moot Hall opposite, were hundreds of demonstrators. They were held back by the fence of fixed bayonets and at one o'clock, after over three hours of mounting tension, the 'Proclamation in the Act for preventing Tumults and riotous Assemblies', was solemnly read out. Allen's diary gives his account of the tragic few minutes which followed:

Gateshead House: now hardly more than an alcove in a street wall. Its Tuscan pilasters stand next to Holy Trinity Church and Community Centre, which incorporates features from the original thirteenth-century chapel of St Edmunds.

> *... and soon after, they made a vigorous effort upon our left and broke in upon them; one of the ring-leaders seized the firelock of a man of Captain Blomberg's company, turned upon the man and shot him dead upon the spot; at the same time, Ensign Hart was shot by a pistol from one of the mob, upon which the word of command was given to fire.* William Allen, 9 March 1761

History is seldom written by its victims and no comparable account has survived from any rioter. When the pall of greasy smoke from the Brown Bess volley cleared, the protesting jeers of the crowd had given way to the cries of their wounded. Allen surveyed what he aptly called 'a spectacle that hurt humanity', which after two centuries has lost none of its power to shock. Its final death toll comprised of two soldiers and forty-nine civilians, two of whom were pregnant women.

> *Rise, Spirit of the Coal! And to mine aid*
> *Usher the Genii of the cavous drift;*
> *And let thy votary, of no harm afraid,*
> *Explore each hollow cavern, rent, and rift;*
> *Shew him the terrors of thy reign let loose,*
> *And help him with the siege of Friar's Goose.* Anonymous, 1832

Friar's Goose, Gateshead: from an industrial heartland and flashpoint of unrest, only the hulk of an 1820s pit engine house remains.

Discontent seethed on into another century. Mass protest was transferred to the industrial scene but the authorities continued to respond to it with sword and musket.

To the alarm of the coal owners, workmen from both counties had banded together to form one union of 'United Colliers' led by lay preacher Thomas Hepburn and in 1832 the vast coalfields of Northumberland and Durham were in turmoil. Strikes to ameliorate appalling working conditions became increasingly vociferous and despite Hepburn's call for restraint were backed by brute force as collieries came under attack and their machinery was smashed. The authorities reacted in kind and rattled the sabre, turning mining districts into military camps:

> *For some time detachments of the regular troops, horse and foot, assisted by parties of Colonel Bell's Cavalry and Foot Yeomanry, were stationed in the neighbourhood of Wallsend; sentries constantly patrolled the immediate locality of certain pits for the protection of the engines and the premises, and the men who were at work; each night the country was scoured by squadrons of cavalry in various directions.* Richard Fynes, 1873.

A war in the North had broken out again and its first pistol shots were heard at Hetton colliery in Durham when the families of striking miners were evicted from their tied cottages, to be replaced by imported 'blackleg' labour. This grim work, shifting 'chairs, table, dresser, bedstead, old or new', was accomplished by a police force from London, armed special constables and magistrates who could call on the locally formed Yeomanry for even more support. The services of this particular militia force, disparagingly nicknamed 'the noodles', were soon requested. After Hetton had been cleared the authorities progressed to Sheriff Hill in Gateshead and east of Newcastle to the village of Friar's Goose, with its coal pit and a chemical works which was rapidly expanding along the bank of the River Tyne.

The 'sullen silent thought' of the colliers at Friar's Goose as they watched their possessions being thrown on to carts became unendurable and a pitched

Most of Jarrow Slake has been reclaimed for modern industrial use, but enough lingers on to picture its troubled past.

battle broke out. Fired on by their own snatched weapons and pelted with 'brickbats, stones and other missiles' which caused several serious wounds, the police hastily withdrew to safer ground. Hindered at every opportunity by miners along his route, a police messenger 'without his hat, with a huge cut in his face, and with one of his ribs broken' eventually galloped into the barracks at Newcastle to deliver a rescue plea. But when the soldiery arrived at Friar's Goose its 'Coaly Army' of colliers had dispersed and the Rector of Gateshead had no cause to read the Riot Act which he carried with him.

'The battle of Friar's Goose' was over but the authorities, unable to closely identify its participants, arrested about forty men and women at random from the neighbourhood and herded them into Newcastle gaol for committal to trial at Durham Assizes. Guarded by the cavalry, they were taken to Durham Prison, and then into the ferment rode Nicholas Fairless.

On 11 June 1832, county magistrate Fairless, travelling alone on the turnpike which skirted the bleak marsh flats of Jarrow Slake, was waylaid by two pitmen. Precisely what occurred afterwards has been a source of conjecture ever since. Perhaps the strikebound colliers were begging and an argument arose in which the strongly opinionated Fairless would tolerate no insolence. The sprightly seventy-one-year-old was a tireless member of the local judiciary and in 1831 was instrumental in quelling riots at South Shields and Hebburn. He was reviled by many, a pillar of the establishment whom Ralph Armstrong and William Jobling now had the opportunity to topple on an isolated road.

During the hue and cry that followed the discovery of the fatally injured magistrate, Jobling was quickly apprehended, but his supposed accomplice, believed to have escaped abroad, was never traced and no one appears to have been tempted by the sizeable reward offered for his capture.

In a murder trial at Durham in which the illiterate Jobling had to conduct his own defence, Judge Parke ascribed the crime to 'the melancholy consequences of that combination of workmen'. Such organisations he believed were 'alike injurious to the public interest and to the interests of those persons concerned in them'. Although the dying Fairless had cleared Jobling of participation in the actual assault and five men had sworn to the accused's previous good character, it took just sixteen minutes for the jury to return their guilty verdict.

> I trust in God that death will operate as it is intended to, as a warning to all others and deter them from following the example of your crime. Justice Sir James Parke, 1 August 1832

Throughout the execution which followed, the hapless Jobling behaved with dignity, protesting his innocence as he 'walked firmly to the drop.' Whether he was an unpardonable criminal or a class martyr, his subsequent degradation provided another hurtful 'spectacle' to haunt the North.

The long-practised gibbeting of criminals, abolished in 1828, was restored by a government unsettled by the social upheaval of the preceding years.

Covered in pitch and encased in a riveted iron cage, Jobling's corpse was hung in chains. To sink it into the Slake's deep mud, the gibbet was fixed into a massive stone. Its one and a half ton base was washed over by the tidal river and it was erected close to the scene of the crime where it remained always within sight of the Jobling family cottage.

After three weeks and four days, however, 'persons yet unknown' risked transportation to put a welcome end to the grisly show. Both gibbet and body were removed, probably by Jobling's fellow mineworkers, a 'spirited set of men', who were rumoured to have then buried their comrade at sea or in the nearby churchyard of Jarrow St Paul's.

The ritual of Jobling's death and gibbeting was a savage postscript to that particular bout of militant agitation. Hungry and demoralised, the miners abandoned their strike and where their masters would have them back, returned humbly to the pithead. The colliers' visionary leader Thomas Hepburn was allowed no such consideration. Expelled from his trade, he was forced to seek menial work and his infant union, almost smothered at birth, took another generation to revive. Its historic sites of struggle and loss, like the protest in Hexham before them, have no markers to commemorate them. But other great sacrifices of recent conflicts are frequently recalled in crafted stone.

No less than any region, the North-East paid the ultimate price in the global wars of modern times, and the counties of Northumberland and Durham are scattered with memorials to its lost generations. Across both counties from city to the smallest village, the legions of northern dead who perished in two vast conflagrations of the twentieth century are grandly remembered. One simple monument attracts scant attention, however. It does not honour a local man but is as poignant and significant as the finest municipal example.

A mist-wreathed night in March 1918 was the ideal condition for a German bombing raid on the north-east coast. Although the dreadful war of attrition in the trenches across Belgium and northern France was then lurching towards a final blood-soaked phase, and Zeppelin attacks on mainland

> *Our lives are not our own. They belong to our country.*
> Sergeant Pilot Joyce, 1918

Britain had ceased, air raid precautions against the long-range Gotha bomber which replaced it remained in force. Enemy activity was reported over Hartlepool on the evening of 13 March, and ponderous machines flown by the Royal Flying Corps lumbered into the air. One of them, an F.E.2b piloted by Londoner Sergeant Arthur Joyce, would never return to its base.

Both British and German aircrew had good reason to fear the F.E.2b. Virtually obsolete at its introduction in 1915, the biplane nevertheless performed well in action, but in crash landings, apart from the usual peril of fire, the rear-mounted engine block of the two-seat aircraft had a lethal tendency to break loose and hurtle forward into the pilot's compartment. On that fateful night in 1918, such a disastrous combination proved fatal for the unfortunate Joyce.

After the 'all clear' was sounded at 10.30 pm, the monotonous droning of

An F.E.2b 'pusher' biplane, built by the Royal Aircraft Factory, preparing for a night flight. On his last mission in March 1918, Sergeant Pilot Joyce flew unaccompanied and the nose of his aircraft was weighted with sandbags. By permission of the Trustees of the Imperial War Museum, London.

Loud Terrace, Annfield Plain: roadside tribute to Sergeant Pilot Joyce. The upper part of the terrace was added after the First World War.

The monument dedicated to Sergeant Joyce and 'all ranks of the Royal Air Forces who gave their lives that this country may remain free.' In a cruel twist of fate, Joyce's son, aged twenty-two, was lost in action flying over Germany in 1940.

his Beardmore engine was heard above Annfield Plain, a mining community in north-west Durham. Ground fog prevented Joyce, flying without an observer, from locating the landing strip and his aircraft spiralled down, low enough for jets of flame to be seen spitting from its exhaust. Dropping signalling flares as he went, he then levelled out for an attempted landing in a field at the edge of the town. Suddenly the gable end of a terraced street loomed out of the mist and Joyce wrenched at his plane's controls to avoid a collision. To the horror of onlookers, the stricken craft turned over and plunged to earth in a ditch opposite Loud Terrace. Would-be rescuers bravely ran towards the wreckage but were held back as the fuel tank exploded into flames. When finally dragged from the smouldering wreck, the burnt and battered pilot was beyond help. Attempting to offer some consolation to the relatives of Sergeant Joyce, the Coroner later stressed that his death was instantaneous; caused by a blow from the radiator and not the subsequent fire.

This accident may pale into insignificance when compared to the carnage then taking place on the Western Front. Yet for the people of Annfield Plain, Sergeant Joyce somehow became a symbol of greater suffering. They took his loss to their hearts.

Even before the inquest was concluded, subscriptions were collected to honour a man who was a stranger in their midst. Similarly, one of the inquiry witnesses was moved by the dramatic events of 13 March to compose a eulogy of praise with Joyce as fallen hero and 'gallant soul' when 'the Huns were abroad.' A swell of jingoistic patriotism, so characteristic of that ghastly conflict, had become focused on the untimely death of a luckless airman. Yet the outpouring of sentiment was no doubt genuine, inspired also by what was regarded to be his supreme act of self-sacrifice. Wreaths were laid by the roadside where Joyce perished and shortly afterwards a more permanent reminder began to take shape. There it remains by a bus stop on the old main road which climbs Loud Hill towards Consett. Its dignified obelisk and surround easily escape the motorist's fleeting glance.

Annfield Plain has been whimsically described as 'a place where no one needs to go', which is certainly untrue, not least with regard to the Joyce monument. Facing Loud Terrace, Joyce's almost apologetic war memorial is a fitting tribute to the commonplace heroism of warfare. Like many other brave acts by ordinary men across the centuries of warfare, the courage of Sergeant Joyce momentarily transcended the barbarism of war. In many such special places from Annfield Plain to Flodden and Neville's Cross, we can reflect how the scourge of battle has touched upon the North. And then, as Daniel Defoe said on another of Britain's great battlefields, we may 'give a short sigh to the memory of the dead, and move forward.'

VISITOR GUIDE

Visitors to Northumberland and Durham should be aware that many of its battle sites are on private land and may not be walked over without express permission of the relevant owner. In most cases, however, large tracts of the battlegrounds may be viewed from nearby public footpaths and bridleways for which maps from the Ordnance Survey Landranger and Explorer series are useful companions.

Berwick, the hub around which so much of Northumbria's conflict revolved, is a fitting place to begin any battlefield tour. Ringed by splendid Elizabethan ramparts, the town also boasts a Georgian barrack complex. It was designed by Nicholas Hawksmoor and now houses the regimental museum of the King's Own Scottish Borderers, which is open throughout the year. Little survives of Berwick's medieval castle. Passengers alighting on the town's railway platform stand on the site of the castle's Great Hall, but fragments can be seen close to the station and in the nearby riverside park.

Two miles to the north-west of Berwick is Halidon Hill. Its car park and information point can be reached from either the A1 at the playfully named Conundrum or from the A6105. A battlefield trail has opened recently at Conundrum Farm. Continuing west along the River Tweed brings the visitor to the key border fortifications of Norham and Wark. Of mighty Wark only a grassy mound survives but Norham is much more substantial. Now in the care of English Heritage, it is open from Easter until September.

Of all battlefields in Northumberland, Flodden has the best access. Footpaths and viewing areas have been added and the car park at Branxton Hill is well signposted from the A697. Two miles east on the B6354, Ford Castle is now private but good views of it can be had from the adjacent churchyard. Ford's model village and working corn mill are also well worth visiting. One mile to the south on the B6353, at the end of a picturesque village street complete with thatched cottages, is Etal Castle. Its Great Tower and gatehouse guarded by naval cannon are open to the public from April until the end of September. Northumberland's major castles, Bamburgh, Warkworth, Alnwick and Prudhoe share a similar visiting season, although the battlefield monuments surrounding Alnwick can be seen at all times and the public Hulne Park containing Hulne Priory and the magnificent Brizlee Tower should not be missed.

Reidswire lies on the A68 at Carter Bar. The memorial can be found on the brow of the ridge, several hundred yards north-east of the cross-border lay-by and viewing point. Spectacular views are only one reward for its discovery. On the A697, fourteen miles to the south, is Otterburn. Percy's Cross is hidden in a roadside plantation, but it is well signposted and is provided with information panels as well as car parking and a picnic site. From its walled boundary there are extensive views of this legendary nocturnal battleground. In common with most others on this battlefield itinerary, the church at Otterburn is usually locked, but perseverance on the visitor's part and the goodwill of a local key-holder can often produce worthwhile results.

The Cheviot battlefields of Milfield, Yeavering and Homildon are just to the north of Wooler on the A697. Although battle stones associated with these conflicts are on farming land, both can be seen clearly from the public road. Homildon's Red Riggs monument lies on the road's north side in the shadow of Humbleton Hill, whilst the Yeavering monolith, watched over by Yeavering Bell, stands at a field boundary one mile west on the B6351. The attraction of visiting Yeavering Bell, 'the city in the hills', has recently been enhanced by way-markers which lead to the ramparts of this ancient hilltop fort. Hedgeley Moor is eight miles further to the south on the A697 between Wooperton and Powburn. A lay-by and roadside enclosure have been provided to visit Percy's Leap which is on the moor's western edge. The Percy Cross, however, is half a mile further south on the opposite side of the road. It is easily visible from there but if more detailed inspection is desired, the railed monument is close to cottages and the privacy of their occupants should be respected.

A little further exertion is required to discover the other sites of Lancastrian woe. Hexham Levels, although only a few miles from the town centre, is almost entirely rural. The traditional battlefield, in a crook of the Devil's Water, is on private farmland but there is a parking at Letah Wood from which it may be approached. Similarly, Swallowship Hill, the alternative Hexham battle site, may be surveyed from the B6307 and there are rights of way through surrounding woodland which pass the splendid Gothic fancy of Duke's House. To the east, however, the Queen's Cave is well concealed in a gorge at Dipton Wood and will only be discovered by the more intrepid battlefield explorer. Hexham's great Priory Church is always open in a vibrant market-place once witness to more sombre events.

North of the town is the World Heritage site of Hadrian's Wall. On its course is Heavenfield. The ancient battleground is found on the B6318 military road at Mile Castle 26 near Chester's fascinating Roman fort and museum. Heavenfield has good roadside information and parking and the battleground and nearby church of St Oswald's are within easy reach of a public footpath.

Moving east along the Tyne valley on the A695 brings the visitor to Bywell Castle. This once important guardian of the River Tyne is now privately owned. The village has disappeared, but as well as the ruined gatehouse of Ralph Neville's castle, not one but two remarkable Saxon churches remain. Newburn, an even more significant river fording point, is six miles downstream. Over the last few years commendable efforts have been made to raise the profile of this neglected battlefield. Part of the Tyne riverside redevelopment, the Newburn Country Park visitor centre has established an informative exhibition which includes battlefield artefacts. The surrounding site is readily accessible and amply served with interpretation panels. All roads from Newburn lead to the city and Newcastle Keep which opens all year round. It contains an excellent yet barely noticed museum and has rooftop views of the city which alone are worth the small admission charged. Newcastle walls can be toured at all times and during the summer months guided walks are available. To the east on the A185 at Jarrow its ancient monastery of St Paul's is now complemented by 'Bedesworld', a prestigious museum which recreates everyday life during the time of the Northumbrian monk and scholar. The Roman Fort and museum at the river mouth in South Shields have opening times just as generous. 'Arbeia's' impressively rebuilt gatehouse has been recently added to by a reconstruction of a barrack block and the commander's villa.

Crossing the river into County Durham, 'Land of the Prince Bishops', Neville's Cross battlefield straddles the A167 on Crossgate Moor at the entrance to the cathedral city. First-class information panels are provided on road bridges crossing the moor and the monument itself is just off the main crossroad at Crossgate Peth. While much of this major battlefield is shrouded forever by the modern road and the grounds of Durham Johnston Comprehensive School, its western approaches are largely extant. A public footpath cuts through Arbour House Farm, from where the Scottish entanglements as they deployed before battle can be appreciated. Similarly, the site of King David's camp at Bearpark can be reached by several paths from the former colliery one mile to the west. Returning to the city, the visitor will find that the oak doors of its magnificent cathedral are open every day and across Palace Green the castle, now incorporated into Durham University, is open for guided tours. Brancepeth Castle, south-west of the city on the A690, is a private residence but is encircled by rights of way. Before leaving County Durham, Bishopton should not be forgotten. One of Northumbria's best-preserved motte and bailey sites, it lies between the A1(M) and the A177, four miles north-west of Stockton-on-Tees.

GUIDE TO SOURCES AND FURTHER READING

Chronicles

Fantsome, J, *Chronicle of War between the English and the Scots*, translated by
    F Michel (1840).

Fordun, J, *Chronicle of the Scottish Nation*, translated by J Skene (1872).

Froissart, J, *Chronicles*, translated by G Brereton (1968).

Hall, E, *Chronicles* (1547).

Hardyng, J, *Chronicles* (1378–1465).

Holinshed, R, *Chronicles* (1580).

Lanercost Chronicle, translated by H Maxwell (1913).

Simeon, *Chronicle*, translated by J Stephenson (1858).

Stowe, J, *Annales* (1525–1605).

Tacitus, *Agricola and Germany*, translated by A Birley (1999).

Trewe Encountre or Batayle lately don between Englande and Scotlande, edited by
    W Garret (1822).

Historical Background

Anderson, R, *The Violent Kingdom* (2000).

Austin, R, *The Rites of Durham* (1995).

Bede, *The Ecclesiastical History of the English People*, edited by J McClure and
    R Collins (1999).

Burke, J, *History of England* (1974).

Durham, K and McBride, A, *Reivers* (1998).

Fraser, C and Emsley, K, *Northumbria* (1989).

Fraser, G, *The Steel Bonnets* (1986).

Fynes, R, *The Miners of Northumberland and Durham* (1986).

Haythornthwaite, P, *The English Civil War* (1994).

Gooch, L, *Desperate Faction* (1995).

Hugill, R, *Castles of Durham* (1979).

Lomas, R, *North-East England in the Middle Ages* (1992).

Lomas, R, *County of Conflict: Northumberland from Conquest to Civil War* (1996).

Mackay, J, *William Wallace* (1995).

Peddie, J, *Invasion* (1987).

Prebble, J, *The Lion in the North* (1973).

Prestwich, M, *Armies and Warfare in the Middle Ages* (1996).

Stranks, C, *This Sumptuous Church* (1993).

Sykes, J, *Local Records* (1883).

Tuck, J, 'Richard II and the Border Magnates', in *Northern History* 3 (1968).

Tuck, J, 'War and Society in the Medieval North', in *Northern History* 21 (1985).

Young, A, *William Cumin: Border Politics and the Bishopric of Durham 1141–1144*
    (1979).

Battlefield Compilations

Clark, D, *Battlefield Walks: North* (1995).
Graham, F, *Famous Northern Battlefields* (1976).
Robson, J, *Border Battles and Battlefields* (1897).
Sadler, J, *Battle for Northumbria* (1988).
Seymour, W, *Battles in Britain 1066–1746* (1997).

Specific Battles and Campaigns

Anderson, R, *The Battle of Newburn* (1975).
Barr, N, *Flodden* (2003).
Brown, C, *The Second Scottish Wars of Independence 1332–1336* (2002).
Charlesworth, D, 'The Battle of Hexham, 1464', in *Archaeologia Aeliana* (1952).
Corfe, T, 'The Hexham Riot', in *The Town of Old Hexham* (2002).
Favver, *The Siege and Storming of Newcastle* (1899).
McNamee, C, 'William Wallace's Invasion of Northern England in 1297', in *Northern History* 26 (1990).
Melia, S, *The Battle of Newburn Ford 1640* [undated].
Nicholson, R, 'The Siege of Berwick 1333', in *Scottish Historical Review* 40 (1961).
Rollason, D and Prestwich, M (eds), *The Battle of Neville's Cross 1346* (1998).
Scammell, J, 'Robert I and the North of England', in *English Historical Review* 73 (1958).
Tomlinson, W, 'Jean Bart's Descent on the Coast of Northumberland in 1691', in *Archaeologia Aeliana* (1900).
Tyson C, 'The Battle of Otterbourne: When and where was it fought?', in *War and Border Societies in the Middle Ages* (1992).
White, R, *The History of the Battle of Otterburn* (1857).

Regional Guides and Histories

Andrews, W, *Bygone Durham* (1898).
Charleton, R, *Charleton's History of Newcastle upon Tyne* (1950).
Dodd, J, *The History of Spennymoor* (1992).
Mee, A, *Northumberland* (1969).
Mee, A, *Durham* (1990).
Graham, F, *Northumbria's Lordly Strand* (1974).
Manders, F, *A History of Gateshead* (1973).
Pevsner, N, *County Durham* (1990).
Pevsner, N, *Northumberland* (1992).
Thorold, H, *County Durham* (1980).
Tomlinson, W, *Comprehensive Guide to Northumberland* (1985).

INDEX